YOUR
ASTROLOGICAL
COMPASS

Navigating Life's Great Cycles

BY
ALICE LOFFREDO

INKWATER PRESS

PORTLAND • OREGON
INKWATERPRESS.COM

*Scan this QR Code
to learn more about
this title*

Cover Illustration by Amanda Ansorge
Cover and interior design by Masha Shubin

Publisher: Inkwater Press | www.inkwaterpress.com

Paperback
ISBN-13 978-1-59299-951-4 | ISBN-10 1-59299-951-4

Kindle
ISBN-13 978-1-59299-952-1 | ISBN-10 1-59299-952-2

ePub
ISBN-13 978-1-59299-953-8 | ISBN-10 1-59299-953-0

Printed in the U.S.A.
All paper is acid free and meets all ANSI standards for archival quality paper.

1 3 5 7 9 10 8 6 4 2

For Don –

For sharing his life with me...
and with you.

and for you, too —

Alice Loffredo
December 1, 2021

i thank You God for most this amazing
day: for the leaping greenly spirits of trees
and a blue true dream of sky; and for everything
which is natural which is infinite which is yes

e. e. cummings

ACKNOWLEDGEMENTS

T HE EXPERIENCES AND LESSONS AND PEOPLE OF A LIFETIME COLLABO-rated in the creation of this book. I offer my heartfelt thanks and appreciation to them all:

The astrologers and teachers and guides and gurus. As always, I play the role of middle-man, taking the wisdom and ideas and insights I have been privileged to acquire from others, and translating and communicating it all to an audience that might not have happened upon it otherwise. As many of their names and works as I can remember are found in these pages and its Bibliography.

Steven Forrest. This time you get an entry of your own. Your voice is the strongest in the astro-choir that backs up my own, and I am so grateful for your guidance, support and encouragement. A special thanks for taking the time in the midst of your incredible schedule to read *Compass* and write its Foreword.

Family and friends and clients and students. The hand-holders and cheerleaders and way-lighters, all. These pages are enriched and informed by your contribution to my life and my work. I cannot list you all by name, for fear of omitting even a single one. Just know that I have received from you all much more than I have ever been able to give or share. Still, some names simply must be named:

- My daughters Sasha and Nikki and my darling granddaughter, Lulu. Thanks for letting me share a glimpse into these beautiful lives that every day inspire and warm my own.

- My sister Claudia, who's shared all but three years of this life with me and has always been in my corner.

- My niece Amanda, who generously contributed the best of her extraordinary talents to create the cover illustration.

- Helen, my very own Book Angel helpmate who flew away to Maryland when her husband's job moved but, thanks to the wonders of modern technology, flutters ever-close with her indispensable helping hands and support.

- Corinda, who believes in my work and helped me shine up the manuscript and navigate the complexities of the publishing world that she herself swims in with such ease and success.

- And, finally, Don. There are adventures we might not ever experience without the love and companionship of one special person. In my life, that person is Don, who in the very act of living his own life in his own way enhances and enriches the unfolding of my own. I'm so glad that you're getting a chance to meet him in these pages. Thanks again, Don!

TABLE OF CONTENTS

ACKNOWLEDGEMENTS vii

FOREWORD xiii

INTRODUCTION – YOUR SPIRIT'S ANATOMY xvii

CHAPTER 1 – PATTERNS AND PASSAGES: THE
SYMBOLISM OF THE BIRTH CHART 1
The Natal Birth Chart...2
The Planets...2
Patterns: Connections in the Natal Birth Chart........................4
Passages: The Evolving Horoscope 6
Life Timeline..8

CHAPTER 2 – SATURN: YOUR ASTROLOGICAL
PERSONAL TRAINER..9
Saturn 9
The Saturn Cycle... 10
Your Own Saturn Return Times and Checkpoints....................14
Saturn Return Chart 15
Saturn Return Worksheet...16
Saturn Checkpoints 18

CHAPTER 3 – ADULTHOOD: THE FIRST SATURN RETURN.....19
Alice at 29 20
Don at 29 21
The Cycle of Preparation: Saturn...23
The First Saturn Return 25
The Moon 26
The Progressed Lunar Cycle...27
The Cycle of Preparation: The Moon 28

Alice's and Don's Karmic Report Cards 30
   Alice's First Saturn Return Report Card 31
   Don's First Saturn Return Report Card 33
Entr'acte: My Child, the Poster Child – Sasha, Age 28 35

CHAPTER 4 – HALFTIME: THE MIDLIFE TRANSITS 38
   Alice at 44 39
   Don at 44 42
Uranus 46
The Uranus Cycle 47
Neptune 50
The Neptune Cycle 52
Saturn 55
Alice's and Don's Mid-Term Report Cards 57
   Alice's Mid-Term Report Card 57
   Don's Mid-Term Report Card 59
Entr'acte: My Child, the Poster Child – Nikki, Age 43 62

CHAPTER 5 – SECOND SPRING: THE SECOND SATURN
RETURN 65
The Transition Years 66
   Alice at 59 67
   Don at 59 69
Saturn 71
Jupiter 75
The Jupiter Cycle 76
The Grand Sextile 78
Uranus Redux 80
Alice's and Don's Second Saturn Return Report Cards 81
   Alice's Second Saturn Return Report Card 81
   Don's Second Saturn Return Report Card 84
Alice and Don: A Very Good Life 87

EPILOGUE 91
Through the Looking Glass 91

Afterword – A True Story...93
Prologue: The Circle of Life 94

THE PLANETARY PLAYBOOK...97
Life Timeline...98
Get Read 99
Make Time for Good Time..99
Put These Quotes On Your Refrigerator Door 101
Take A Trip Down Memory Lane................................. 102
Ask Good Questions... Find Good Answers. 103
Create a Ritual 110
Write an Ethical Will (Second Saturn Return) 112
Look for Help to Show Up...115

APPENDIX...117
More About The Birth Chart..117
Glossary...125
Bibliography 130
Chapter Notes 133

AUTHOR PROFILE..135

FOREWORD

WHEN I WAS A YOUNG ASTROLOGER STILL WET BEHIND THE EARS, I would sometimes find myself in the awkward position of counseling somebody's grandmother about getting old. For her, this was presumably a lot like getting romantic tips from a virgin. I am sure I tripped over my ignorance on many occasions. How could it be otherwise? How could a 27 year old possibly know what it felt like to be 65? On the face of it, to even try seems like sheer hubris.

But I had an ace in the hole: astrology itself. Human beings have been watching the heavens for millennia, relating the planetary cycles to their own experiences.

In talking to that grandmother, I stood on the shoulders of my astrological ancestors. Many of them had been elders, who of course started out life as babies and thus experienced the whole journey from cradle to grave. Some had been generous enough to record what they had learned, adding it to the treasure-house of astrological literature. Some were men, some were women. Some were Europeans or Americans. Some were Chinese or Indian or Mayan, and so on.

Most human cultures have practiced some form of astrology

for at least part of their histories. As a young astrologer, that entire self-correcting legacy was at my fingertips. In speaking with that grandmother, I was saved from making a total fool of myself by that precious tradition. Still, now that I am older, I know I am a far better astrologer.

Aging is kinder to astrologers than it is to people in many other professions where youthfulness is more of an advantage. Life naturally teaches us deeper wisdom—or at least it tries pretty hard! Another way to say it is that as we age we inevitably experience more and more of the various kinds of astrological stimuli. What we once read in a book, we now know in our organisms and psyches. This of course adds resonance and authority to the words we might have learned to parrot from the pages of a book. To claim that no one can understand, say, the "black experience" unless they are black grievously under-estimates the power of the human imagination.

But of course if you really want to understand the black experience as profoundly as you can, you don't ask the Pope. It is the same with the astrology of the life-cycle, which Alice Loffredo covers so ably in this book. She's old enough to remember a few Beatles' tunes, and those miles on her existential odometer enrich these pages enormously.

Astrology is both constant and ever-new. It is constant because the laws of astronomy declare that we have all been experiencing pretty much exactly the same patterns of planetary stimulus since the beginning of human history. But astrology is ever-new because human culture keeps re-inventing itself.

Twenty years ago a friend of mine went to hear Van Morrison in concert. When she told me about it later, she said, "He looks the way 45 year old men used to look." I loved that comment. I felt like I knew exactly what she meant. Being 45 in the 1920s was a whole different experience than, say, being 45 today in modern Los Angeles. Biologically, there are indeed certain more-or-less reliable constants in the aging process. But the cultural elements vary wildly. That is why astrology must constantly re-invent itself. It must do that in order to be relevant to actual human experience. For example, as I write these words, Madonna is 52. She is still, in broad terms, taken as a plausible sex goddess. That would have been a hard sell in the 1950s.

Times have changed. Imagine an astrologer today assuming that feeling sexy was simply out of the question for a 52 year old—or assuming that the 16 year old was a blushing virgin. Those assumptions might have worked once, but no longer. This is the kind of thing I mean when I say that astrology, even though its cycles are constant, must constantly be renewed by astrologers who are truly contemporary, truly part of present cultural realities.

Enter Alice Loffredo. In these pages, she is not making a monkey of herself by bending over backwards to be perceived as hip. Blessedly, she is not trying to sound as if she were 25 years younger than she is. <u>But she sounds modern</u>. She is a Baby Boomer facing elder hood. She is not her grandmother. Her voice has the ring of present reality. And it is a helpful voice. Anyone can have experience. Most of us get old. But there is a big difference between digested experience and the kind of experience that just "happens" to someone as they passively watch their hair turn gray.

Alice is never pious about this, but she has clearly lived an examined life. And she has expanded and enhanced her natural wisdom by examining her life through the electron-microscope of astrology.

In these pages, she offers us the great gift of sharing what she has learned. She has helped renew astrology, feeding its endless need to update itself. I wish her many more years in this world and I hope that before she casts off the mortal coil she is able to turn her scrutiny onto the astrological signposts she has not yet lived long enough to experience. That is a gift I happily anticipate.

Steven Forrest
Borrego Springs, California

YOUR SPIRIT'S ANATOMY

*"Human beings construct meaning as spiders make webs.
This is how we survive, (it is) our primary evolutionary business."*

CATHERINE BATESON [1]

AT AGE TWENTY-NINE, PRINCE SIDDHARTHA GAUTAMA LEFT HIS WIFE and his son, and a life of royal luxury to seek enlightenment and became the Buddha. Centuries later, at that same age, Eckhart Tolle experienced a crisis of consciousness that almost ended his life but led, ultimately, to the writing of his benchmark book, *The Power of Now*.

At age forty-two, Rosa Parks refused to obey a bus driver's order to give up her seat to make room for a white passenger and became a civil rights rallying-point and legend.

In 1789, George Washington became the first President of the United States at age fifty-seven, and a hundred years later, at the same time of life, Claude Monet started painting the water lilies on his property in Giverny, France.

In all likelihood, none of these people had even the slightest awareness of astrology but, guided by the planetary master teacher Saturn, they were navigating important astrological passages that

---

[1] See **Chapter Notes** for numbered sources and references

occur in each of our lives. These milestones are the subject matter of *Your Astrological Compass*.

More than forty million **Baby Boomers** have started to arrive at the third of these periods. They are entering a time of life when people often look back to examine the patterns and meaning of its unfolding, to observe and try to understand how ancient cycles of growth and evolution are repeated in the unique context of their own biographical history. They applaud successes and linger in the recollection of happy moments. They lament untaken opportunities and misguided – or unguided – decisions, wishing they could have seen the patterns that are clear now, but were invisible to them at the time: Why did so many relationships end the same way, in dissent, anger, and hurt feelings? Why was it always *me* who was passed over when it came to recognition or a big promotion? Why didn't I see financial disaster coming before it showed up for the third time? Why, oh why, did I always shoot myself in the foot with the same self-defeating behavior, just at the brink of success? They wonder: Is it all over? I can't go back, can I? Maybe if I take enough supplements, get a little "work" done, and look into the latest research on the human growth hormone, I can cheat time long enough to rewrite some of those stories and get them right.

But maybe there's another way, one that allows a person to arrive at life's important passages empowered to live with awareness, to see the potential and challenges of patterns waiting to unfold. Could there be a resource that helps a person live in the opportunities and graces of who they are instead of trying to cling to what once was, but is no longer relevant; one that offers a way to find answers to questions about how best to use the time that stretches out into the future?

The great good news is that there is.

Your Spirit's Anatomy. From the highest echelons of research and technology to the daily gaze into the mirror as we perform our morning grooming routines, there are many, many ways to measure and support the state of our physical body and our progress in the outer world of experience and accomplishment. However, there are precious few that track and guide the status and growth of the spirit, that eternal part of each one of us that knows no boundaries in space or time, that part of us whose evolution weaves the patterns of our biographical lives. But there are some, and astrology is one of them.

Using the rich, broad strokes of its objective symbolism, astrology paints the patterns of a lifetime for all of us in a framework that allows for precise customization based on the nature and potential of each unique individual. It helps us understand who we are at a deep, authentic level, allows us to anticipate opportunities for learning and growth, and can help us avoid pitfalls that might hold us back. And astrology can help us decide how and when to allocate all our resources – personal and material – in the best possible way. Using its wise guidance, we can create new scales of meaning to measure what's important and then, calling on what we've learned and experienced so far, move confidently and optimistically into the possibilities of the next phase of life, making the most of each of its moments.

And the news only gets better. At every significant generational passage – adulthood, the mid-life years, and the dawning, at around age sixty, of what astrologer Erin Sullivan calls the period of the "Meaningful Return to the Self"–– the Universe dishes up to each of us a great convergence of planetary energetic potential. Used consciously, that energy can help us write the next chapter of our life's storyline in the best possible way.

Welcome to *Your Astrological Compass*, the guide and handbook for making the most of these times. Let's get going...

Your Astrological Compass

Navigating Life's Great Cycles

PATTERNS AND PASSAGES: THE SYMBOLISM OF THE BIRTH CHART

"It is the stars as not known to science that I would know."

HENRY DAVID THOREAU [1]

A MANDALA IS A SYMBOLIC PATTERN, USUALLY CIRCULAR IN SHAPE, THAT represents a depiction of the Universe. It is a symbol of wholeness and integration. Your astrological **birth chart** or **horoscope**, frozen for a lifetime at the exact time and place of your birth, is a mandala of energetic connections representing your *personal* universe. It's as if a photographer was standing right on the delivery table when you were born, holding some kind of mega-magical-camera pointed straight up to the sky. "Click!" There it is, an incredibly complex web of symbols representing your personality and its various qualities and abilities; your very own planetary energetic picture captured for a lifetime – in the birth chart and, more importantly, in you. The chart also indicates the kinds of experiences and lessons and opportunities to make choices and decisions that you might encounter in order to fulfill that potential, and gives a clue or two as to some roadblocks that might try to hold you back. In other words, the horoscope is one phenomenal tool that you can use to write the best story you possibly can of this particular lifetime: to understand why you are the way you are; to explore your life purpose; to figure out the next best step as your life unfolds.

THE NATAL BIRTH CHART

The birth chart is composed of three groups of symbols:

- *Planets.* The ten planets represent basic types of energy found in everyone. Mercury, for example, represents how we learn and think and communicate. The Moon describes how we experience our emotions and intuition.

- *Signs.* The twelve signs act like filters applied to the planets' energies, modifying and "coloring" their expression. Cancer is a watery, emotional, intuitive sign and Gemini is an airy, intellectual, communicative sign.

- *Houses.* Each of these twelve pie-shaped segments of the perfectly circular field of the birth chart represents certain life experiences. For example, the Seventh House represents themes having to do with all kinds of partnerships, including marriage.

There's a lot more about all this in the "More About the Birth Chart" in the **Appendix.** The article offers information about the signs and houses, and describes how the birth chart is constructed. The **Appendix** also includes a Glossary of terms that are **bolded and italicized** the first time they appear in these pages.

THE PLANETS

The chart that follows contains thumbnail descriptions of each of the planets, which are the primary focus of this book. Italicized names designate the planets that play key roles. Since all astrological symbols are neutral, but can be expressed in either positive or negative ways depending on our free will and choice, I'll alert you to some of the downside for each.

· · ✦ THE PLANETS ✦ · ·

Name	Description	Negative Expression
Sun	Our essential, fundamental nature and identity. The energy we are here to experience, learn about, model for others, and contribute. Our capacity for self-expression. Our ego and selfhood in the most positive sense. The part of us, regardless of gender, that is associated with male energy (*the animus*).	Egotism. Selfishness. Arrogance. Self-satisfaction. Insensitivity.
Moon	Our emotions. How we nurture and are nurtured. Instinct and intuition. Sensitivity and receptivity. The Unconscious. The part of us, regardless of gender, that is associated with female energy (*the anima*).	Moodiness. Emotional self-indulgence. Over-sensitivity. Unconscious behavior that runs the show to our own or someone else's detriment.
Mercury	How we think and communicate. Intelligence and reasoning ability. The way we transmit and receive information.	Intellectual snobbism. Flightiness and fickleness. Superficiality.
Venus	Love. Affection. Sociability. Charm. Our response to beauty. Diplomacy and compromise.	Vanity. Apathy. Self-indulgence. Indolence.

· ◆ ◆ THE PLANETS ◆ ◆ ·

NAME	DESCRIPTION	NEGATIVE EXPRESSION
Mars	Physical energy. Courage. Initiation. Self-assertiveness and the power of will. The physical part of sexuality.	Selfishness. Willfulness. "Me First" attitude. Rage. Aggressiveness.
Jupiter	Abundance. Expansion. Generosity. Growth. Faith. Prosperity. Optimism. Luck.	Extravagance. Pretense. Self-indulgence. Excess.
Saturn	Authority. Responsibility. Ambition. Discipline. The urge for security and safety. What we need to learn. The role model for success.	Coldness. Limitation. Suppression of emotion. Dreary, hard work.
Uranus	Uniqueness and individuality. Sudden, unforeseen change. Brilliance. Spontaneity.	Extreme eccentricity. Insensitivity. Touchiness. Disruption.
Neptune	Direct contact with the Divine. Spirituality. Dreaminess. Creativity. Intuition. Imagination. Vision.	Escapism. Addiction. Confusion. Apathy. Deception. Denial.
Pluto	Intensity. Depth. Transformation. Our ability to confront the "dark" in whatever form it takes, and heal it.	Power plays. Violence. Obsession. "End justifies the means." Jealousy. Manipulation.

PATTERNS: CONNECTIONS IN THE NATAL BIRTH CHART

The planets connect – or don't – to each other in angular relationships called ***aspects***. Aspects are based on how much distance there is between the particular planets that are connected, and describe how the energy moves between these planets. We'll be encountering most of the major aspects in *Your Astrological Compass*. They are:

- **Squares*** and **Oppositions***. These are challenging, and can bring tension and stress. They feel like you do when you've tried for the eighth time to put together the kit for a backyard swing set and the smooth side of the slide is *still* facing in the wrong direction. However, challenge and stress provide motivation for growth and change.

- **Conjunctions***. These are created when two or more planets are right next to, or even on top of, each other. Conjunctions fuse the energies of the planets involved, creating an intense powerhouse of energetic potential.

- **Sextiles*** and **Trines***. These create ease and flow, like that feeling you have when you wake up on a bright, sunny morning after a good night's sleep and can't wait to see what the world is going to deliver for that day. Smooth, optimistic flow helps us secure progress and enjoy its satisfactions, replenishing us so we can take up the challenge of growth again.

For example, the planet Mercury (how we learn and think and communicate) in flowing aspect (a trine, for example) to Uranus (brilliance and originality) thinks quickly, comes up with lots of original ideas, and communicates those ideas in an interesting, lively manner that invites audience attention. Mercury, in tense, challenging aspect (a square, let's say) to that same Uranus, can indicate a mind that's abuzz 24/7, coming up with ideas so far out of the box that only the person thinking them can comprehend or relate to them. Mercury combined (in conjunction) with Uranus

---

*These terms are defined specifically in the Glossary.

can spontaneously come up with the totally new, bright idea that revolutionizes (a true Uranian word if ever there was one, by the way) existing thought on a subject, like Copernicus' breakthrough idea of a solar-centered Universe.

Take the ten planets. Factor in the twelve signs and twelve houses, and the 360 degrees of the birth chart's circle. The resulting combinations and variations are virtually endless, adding up to what astrologer Steven Forrest calls the "underlying unity behind the shifting, changing energies (of life)," [2] which takes us right to our next topic.

PASSAGES: THE EVOLVING HOROSCOPE

The planets are always moving. Right from your first breath, they continue on their way, each passing through the twelve signs of the **zodiac** at its own pace. The Moon completes the circuit approximately every twenty-eight days, changing its sign every two and one-half days. Pluto, at the other extreme, spends up to twenty *years* in each sign, and will pass through only a few of them in the course of a lifetime.

A *cycle* is the time it takes for a planet to return to its starting place, its unchanging position in your natal birth chart. That arrival at home plate is called a **return**. Jupiter takes twelve years to complete a cycle, Saturn almost thirty. Some cycles will never be completed in a lifetime – Neptune's is about 168 years long, Pluto's, more than 220 – but within that planet's cycle, important times are recognized.

As the planets move in their cycles through the zodiac, they make aspects to the natal planets that are in their unchanging positions in the birth chart. Those energetic connections are called **transits,** and when they are happening, a window of time is opened with opportunity for growth and change. Think of transits as moving aspects. Some are flowing, others are challenging. Interpreting those evolving energetic relationships is in large part how astrologers know what kinds of experiences, lessons, opportunities and challenges an individual is encountering at any given time. The Universe does not judge certain transits to be good, and others to be bad. Each has its important purpose in guiding us to the best of all possible lives.

Most times, transits occur when a moving planet connects to a planet other than itself, but sometimes the connection is made between the moving planet and its own "natal self," sitting in our birth chart where it was at the moment of our birth. As we will see, those planet-to-itself transits often mark important passages in our evolving biographical lives.

So there you have it, the barest of bones: ten planets, wired into meaningful energetic connections, both natally, and going forward as time unfolds.

LIFE TIMELINE

This simple timeline identifies the key evolutionary periods that are the subject of *Your Astrological Compass*. You'll be learning about the planetary events in the pages that follow, so don't worry about them for now. A more detailed chart is found at the start of **The Planetary Playbook**, which follows the **Epilogue** towards the end of the book.

· · ✦ LIFE TIMELINE ✦ · ·

AGE (APPROXIMATE)	LIFE EVENT	PLANETARY EVENT
27-29	Adulthood Begins	Progressed Lunar Return
		First Saturn Return
40-44	Midlife Passage	Uranus Opposite Uranus
		Neptune Square Neptune
		Saturn Opposite Saturn
58-62	The Cycle of the Meaningful Return to the Self Begins	Second Saturn Return
		Jupiter Return
		Grand Sextile
		Uranus Square Uranus
Looking Ahead		
Age 72	Mid-Cycle	Saturn Opposite Saturn
		Jupiter Return
Ages 84-88	Cycle of Individuation Culminates	Uranus Return
		Third Saturn Return
		Jupiter Return
		Neptune Opposite Neptune

CHAPTER 2

SATURN: YOUR ASTROLOGICAL PERSONAL TRAINER

*"Father Time is not always a hard parent, and though
he tarries for none of his children, often lays his hands
lightly upon those who have used him well.*

CHARLES DICKENS
BARNABY RUDGE

♄

SATURN

· · ◆ DESCRIPTION ◆ · ·

Represents: Authority. Responsibility. Ambition. Discipline. What we need to learn. The role model for success.

Negative Expression: Coldness. Limitation. Suppression of emotion. Dreary, hard work.

Role: The Karmic Teacher. The Authoritarian Parent. The Boss. The Elder. Father Time.

WE CAN LEARN A LOT ABOUT SATURN FROM THE SIMPLE FACT THAT ITS astrological symbol, or *glyph* – ♄ – is taken from the alchemical symbol for lead, the heaviest element on our planet. There's nothing more solid, more down-to-earth than lead, and those qualities are core to the description of Saturn's energy. In other words, this is a realistic, no-nonsense, heavy-duty planet. Saturn likes to see defined, tangible, measurable goals and accomplishments. It likes structure and limits and control, and it stands for responsibility and accountability. "Pie in the sky" promises and ideals are simply not in its realm.

Saturn's job description is to provide us with the ground rules for success on this earthly plane, so that we can release our birth chart's – *i.e.* our life's – potential. In order to do this, Saturn plays two key roles. First, it is the great Karmic Teacher, charged with helping us identify goals, create strategic and tactical plans to achieve them, and be accountable for our progress. Secondly, it represents the archetype of the Authoritarian Parent, the person who, regardless of gender, made sure you did your homework before you watched television; the one that made you dry the dishes and take out the garbage when it was your turn; the one who knew that you played hooky and forged the note – and *grounded* you for it.

In either role, Saturn operates like a personal trainer getting an athlete ready for the Olympics, administering a program designed specifically for each of us, modeling and demanding discipline, hard work, and the achievement of cold, hard results. It measures our progress (or lack of it) and designs rewards and consequences accordingly. Like the alchemists of long ago, Saturn's goal is to take the earthy elements of which we are made, and change them into the gold of our highest potential. But it's each of us that has to be willing to take on the challenge of the curriculum, do the homework, and pass the tests.

THE SATURN CYCLE

Saturn's natal position in our horoscope tells us how and under what circumstances we are likely to learn some of the most important lessons of this lifetime. Let's say you have Saturn in the curious, communicative sign of Gemini, the sign associated with learning and teaching, and that the planet is placed in the area of the birth chart that represents, among other things, higher education and far-away travel. We can surmise that, throughout your lifetime, taking courses that catch your interest (the credits and diplomas are not what's important here) and exposing yourself to the "culture shock" of traveling far from your everyday world, will provide insights and experiences that will shape and enhance your life.

But that's not the *only* way you will learn and grow. Saturn, like all the other planets, continues to move, and will spend approximately two and one half years in each of the other signs and houses, giving you the chance to learn in different ways (signs) and through different types of experiences (houses). For example, when it passes through the sign of Aries (action) in the (Sixth) House of work and health, you might have experiences where you learn about avoiding burn-out on the job.

> **Astrological Rule of Thumb:** The longer a transit or energy passage lasts, the more important it is to the evolutionary growth of the individual.

As we have seen in Chapter 1, each planet moves according to its own unique rhythm. The Moon takes twenty-eight days to move through all the signs and houses and circle the birth chart. At the other extreme, Pluto takes 220 years to cover the same terrain. Somewhere between these two lies Saturn's twenty-nine year cycle, an important amount of time.

After about twenty-nine years, Saturn returns to its unchanging natal position in the birth chart, ending one cycle of growth and development, and launching another. Like any good teacher, Saturn will issue a report card at each of these returns, and then provide the curriculum and marching orders that will help launch the next cycle. At these times, Saturn can bring hidden or repressed issues to play out at the surface of our biographical lives, things we either didn't know we had to look at, and/or situations we have chosen to ignore.

These issues manifest so that we can deal with them in the world of the here and now, in pragmatic, common-sense ways. Saturn ways.

Let's say that you chose to play hooky while Saturn passed through the house of money, and have spent the last several years dancing between the raindrops of financial disaster: borrowing from Peter (read "plastic") to pay Paul (the mortgage company); grabbing 10K out of the kids' college fund to take a ten-day cruise to cheer up your spouse, who's feeling so bad because her sister just got back from a month in Hawaii; cashing in half of the 401K retirement account (penalties be damned, you'll make it up somehow) to replace the family jalopy because you can't get a decent car loan thanks to your horrific credit score. At its return, Saturn may just have to dish up the grace of a job loss to get you out of the juggling act and help you start rebuilding from limited, but solid ground. It's not punishment (though it certainly may feel that way). It's simply the delivery of consequences in alignment with the grade on the report card, delivered in quantities strong and dramatic enough to get your attention. Are these times easy? Of course not. What's more, we live in a society where youth and spontaneity are generally over-valued and over-extended – a culture that equates "serious" with "uncomfortable" and "disciplined" with "boring" or "bad." Get past those judgments, and you can reframe experience as opportunity, push yourself to grow up, and start to make real, perceptible progress toward getting your life on track, no matter what your age.

Of course, the goal is to "Ace" the assignment, and if you pull that off, Saturn is going to come through with rewards of success, stability, and security, in nice, tangible, Saturn-loving form, guaranteeing the best possible start-up for the upcoming cycle. Either way, once we demonstrate that we are ready to do our part through commitment, responsibility, hard work, and self-discipline, Saturn will help us formulate the solutions and goals, and develop plans for their execution.

As to the report card you'll actually get? The choice, as always, is yours.

Three great astrological life cycles, launched from Saturn's natal position in the birth chart, or its subsequent returns to that position every twenty-nine years, frame the story of our evolving lifetimes:

- *Saturn at Birth: The Cycle of Preparation (ages 0-29)*, during which we acquire (or don't) the skills, experiences, and information we need in order to assume the full responsibilities and privileges of adulthood.

- *The First Saturn Return: The Cycle of Adulthood (ages 30-59)*, during which we acquit those responsibilities, enjoy those privileges, and make a contribution to the world we live in...or don't. During this cycle, we all experience the *Midlife Transits,* another important marking point along our developmental way.

- *The Second Saturn Return: The Cycle of the Meaningful Return to the Self (age 60 forward)*, during which our focus shifts inward, to living the life that reflects our own unique authenticity and potential.

At each of the Saturn returns, at

Your Astrological Compass describes the energetic passages that occur for *everyone* at the Saturn Returns, and at Midlife. Because they are the same for everyone in the same approximate age group, they are called **generational transits.** However, it is more than likely that the moving planets are also affecting your individual birth chart in ways that are unique to you and you alone, ways that might facilitate the energies of the generational passages, and/or challenge them. It is such a good idea to get a professional reading of your horoscope during the times of these huge generational energetic passages, so that you can have the whole picture of what's going on in your own, unique life, and make the most of it.

times of endings and beginnings, other planets will enter the energetic mix. Together, they act like "invisible hands helping (you) along a path (you) need to follow,[1]" bringing opportunities for growth and development, and enjoyment of life. We will meet up with other planets when they make their appearances, but because he is the definer and guardian of the great life cycles, Saturn, whose other name is *Kronos*, the Greek word for "time," deserves his own chapter.

YOUR OWN SATURN RETURN TIMES AND CHECKPOINTS

Knowing when these important passages occur in your own life will help you personalize the information offered in *Compass* and make the most of each of these important milestones. Use the **Saturn Return Chart** and the easy step-by-step worksheets in the next few pages to identify the approximate times of your Saturn Returns and intermediate checkpoints. Of course, the best approach would be to obtain a precisely-calculated birth chart based on the DATE – TIME – PLACE of your birth and have an astrologer determine the exact times for you.

In the **Saturn Return Chart** on the next page:

- Sign symbols and names are provided for your convenience, but are not required in order to benefit from the information in *"Compass."*

- Date ranges are *very* approximate, especially the beginning and end of each range, when the planet's actual sign may differ from what's listed. This is because Saturn's orbit is elliptical and its movement somewhat irregular,

Once you've identified your approximate Saturn Return and checkpoint information, we're ready to let the sky-show begin – to see how it all plays out in real life.

· · · SATURN RETURN CHART · · ·

BIRTH DATE RANGE	SATURN'S SIGN AND SYMBOL		1ST SATURN RETURN	2ND SATURN RETURN
Mar. 1932 – Jan. 1935	Aquarius	♒	Jan. 1962 – Mar. 1964	Feb. 1991 – Jan. 1994
Feb. 1935 – Apr. 1937	Pisces	♓	Apr. 1964 – Feb. 1967	Feb. 1994 – Mar. 1996
May 1937 – Mar. 1940	Aries	♈	Mar. 1967 – Apr. 1969	Apr. 1996 – May 1998
Apr. 1940 – Apr. 1942	Taurus	♉	May 1969 – June 1971	June 1998 – July 2000
May 1942 – June 1944	Gemini	♊	July 1971 – July 1973	Aug. 2000 – May 2003
July 1944 – July 1946	Cancer	♋	Aug. 1973 – Sept. 1975	June 2003 – July 2005
Aug. 1946 – Sep. 1948	Leo	♌	Oct. 1975 – Nov. 1977	Aug. 2005 – Aug. 2007
Oct. 1948 – July 1951	Virgo	♍	Dec. 1977 – Sept. 1980	Sept. 2007 – Oct. 2009
Aug. 1951 – Oct. 1953	Libra	♎	Oct. 1980 – Nov. 1982	Nov. 2009 – Sept. 2012
Nov. 1953 – Sept. 1956	Scorpio	♏	Dec. 1982 – Nov. 1985	Oct. 2012 – Dec. 2014
Oct. 1956 – Dec. 1958	Sagittarius	♐	Dec. 1985 – Jan. 1988	Jan. 2015 – Dec. 2017
Jan. 1959 – Dec. 1961	Capricorn	♑	Feb. 1988 – Jan. 1991	Jan. 2018 – Mar. 2020
Jan. 1962 – Mar. 1964	Aquarius	♒	Feb. 1991 – Jan. 1994	Apr. 2020 – Feb. 2023
Apr. 1964 – Feb. 1967	Pisces	♓	Feb. 1994 – Mar. 1996	Mar. 2023 – Jan. 2026
Mar. 1967 – Apr. 1969	Aries	♈	Apr. 1996 – May 1998	Feb. 2026 – Mar. 2028
May 1969 – June 1971	Taurus	♉	June 1998 – July 2000	Apr. 2028 – May 2030
July 1971 – July 1973	Gemini	♊	Aug. 2000 – May 2003	June 2030 – June 2032
Aug. 1973 – Sept. 1975	Cancer	♋	June 2003 – July 2005	July 2032 – Aug. 2034
Oct. 1975 – July 1978	Leo	♌	Aug. 2005 – Aug. 2007	Sept. 2034 – Sept. 2036
Aug. 1978 – Sept. 1980	Virgo	♍	Sept. 2007 – Oct. 2009	Oct. 2036 – Aug. 2039
Oct. 1980 – Nov. 1982	Libra	♎	Nov. 2009 – Sept. 2012	Sept. 2039 – Oct. 2041
Dec. 1982 – Nov. 1985	Scorpio	♏	Oct. 2012 – Dec. 2014	Nov. 2041 – Oct. 2044
Dec. 1985 – Jan. 1988	Sagittarius	♐	Jan. 2015 – Dec. 2017	Nov. 2044 – Jan. 2047
Feb. 1988 – Jan. 1991	Capricorn	♑	Jan. 2018 – Mar. 2020	Feb. 2047 – Jan. 2050
Feb. 1991 – Jan. 1994	Aquarius	♒	Apr. 2020 – Feb. 2023	Feb. 2050 – Dec. 2052
Feb. 1994 – Mar. 1996	Pisces	♓	Mar. 2023 – Jan. 2026	Jan. 2053 – Mar. 2055
Apr. 1996 – May 1998	Aries	♈	Feb. 2026 – Mar. 2028	Apr. 2055 – May 2057

This worksheet shows how to find the approximate Saturn Return months for a person born in May 1952.

· · ◆ SATURN RETURN WORKSHEET ◆ · ·

Step	Find...	Instruction	Result
1	**Birth Month and Year**		**May 1952**
2	**Birth Date Range**	Consult Saturn Return Chart.	**Aug. 1951 – Oct. 1953**
3	**Find Number of Months**	Count the months from the beginning of the Birth Date Range to your actual birth month.	**10 months** Aug. – Dec. 1951 (5 months) + Jan. – May 1952 (5 months)
4	**First Saturn Return Date Range**	Consult Saturn Return Chart.	**Oct. 1980 – Nov. 1982**
5	**First Saturn Return Month (Approx.)**	Count the number of months from Step 3 into the date ranges for the 1st Saturn Return.	**July 1981**
6	**Second Saturn Return Date Range**	Consult Saturn Return Chart.	**Nov. 2009 – Sept. 2012**
7	**Second Saturn Return Month (Approx.)**	Count the number of months from Step 3 into the date ranges for the 2nd Saturn Return.	**August 2010**

Use this worksheet to determine your own approximate Saturn Return months.

· · ◆ SATURN RETURN WORKSHEET ◆ · ·

STEP	FIND...	INSTRUCTION	RESULT
1	**Birth Month and Year**		
2	**Birth Date Range**	Consult Saturn Return Chart.	
3	**Find Number of Months**	Count the months from the beginning of the Birth Date Range to your actual birth month.	
4	**First Saturn Return Date Range**	Consult Saturn Return Chart.	
5	**First Saturn Return Month (Approx.)**	Count the number of months from Step 3 into the date ranges for the 1st Saturn Return.	
6	**Second Saturn Return Date Range**	Consult Saturn Return Chart.	
7	**Second Saturn Return Month (Approx.)**	Count the number of months from Step 3 into the date ranges for the 2nd Saturn Return.	
8	**Info when you need it.**	Jot down your Saturn Return months and years, on a piece of paper and use it as a bookmark for *Compass*.	

SATURN CHECKPOINTS

Saturn is a demanding, but fundamentally benevolent taskmaster. It's not like he leaves us adrift on our own for thirty years a time, only to suddenly hold us accountable for exemplary results every three decades. No, like any good teacher, Saturn issues interim reports at the end of every marking period. In Saturn time, this means about every seven and a quarter years when the Karmic Teacher makes important contact with its unchanging natal position in the birth chart. These are times when we can make the adjustments that will keep us from veering too far off course.

SATURN RETURNS AND CHECKPOINTS

The following are the approximate ages when Saturn Returns and checkpoints occur.

First Saturn Return:	29	**Saturn Checkpoints:**	36, 44, 51
Second Saturn Return:	58	**Saturn Checkpoints:**	65, 73, 80
Third Saturn Return	87		

EXTRA CREDIT ACTIVITY: To establish more precise (but still not exact) timing, use the Saturn Return dates you established in the **Worksheet**, and

- add 7 years and 6 months to the *Return* date to establish the first checkpoint;
- add 7 years and 6 months to the *first* checkpoint to find the second checkpoint;
- add 7 years and 6 months to the *second* checkpoint to get the third checkpoint.

Example:

First Saturn Return: July 1981 (from Worksheet example)

First Checkpoint: January 1989

Second Checkpoint: July 1996

Third Checkpoint: January 2004

➔ **Add checkpoint ages and/or dates to your *Compass* bookmark.**

CHAPTER 3

ADULTHOOD: THE FIRST SATURN RETURN

(AGES 27 - 29)

"We tell stories because we can't help it.
We tell stories because we love to entertain and hope to edify...
We tell stories because they save us."

JAMES CARROLL [1]

How CAN YOU GRASP THE BRASS RING OF SHINING OPPORTUNITY WHEN you're on the verge of becoming sixty if you don't know how you got on the merry-go-round in the first place? Regardless of where we may be right now in the timeline of our own life story, looking at important milestones can help us plan for the future and correct course if necessary in the present. So we start with the First Saturn Return, the culmination of the Cycle of Preparation and the launch point of the Cycle of Adulthood.

Arriving at the First Saturn Return, we have had approximately twenty-nine years to get ready to assume the full complement of adult responsibilities and privileges. But before we step fully into that role, we are given the opportunity to evaluate how well we have prepared for it. Important questions need to be asked, and decisions made to assure a successful start for the Cycle of Adulthood. Where were/are you at the age of twenty-nine? What was/is life like for you? If the First Saturn Return is in the past, did you strike out in new directions, or did you move forward in the established path? Was that a good choice?

••••◆••••

As I prepared to put word to paper for this book, I knew I needed to tell a real life story, one that would put flesh and bones to the information I wanted to share. I searched diligently for that story. I reviewed client files and celebrity biographies, and found great richness in both, but at the end of it all, the story I realized I had to tell was my own...and Don's.

ALICE AT 29

In the softening dark of a five o'clock morning, Alice slips out of bed and carefully moves out into the hallway that looks down over an elegant entrance foyer. She passes the closed bedroom doors that line her passage, and makes her way quietly downstairs to the kitchen. She's mindful not to disturb her sleeping family, not only out of consideration, but because she holds precious the solitary hour that awaits her, the only one she will have before this time again tomorrow.

The coffee maker has been set up the night before, and Alice flips it on so it can brew her first cup while she fills the bowls for Rusty and Beau, the two middle-aged, mixed-breed treasures who are her constant companions. They grab a quick mouthful and she opens the back door to let them out to where they'll wander the neighborhood for the next hour, thereby assuring her solitude.

She pours a mug of coffee, splashes in some milk, and settles in at the table. It's still too dark to have any sense of what lies out-side the windows that surround the breakfast nook. Soon enough the sky will lighten and she'll be able to look out over her beloved, well-tended garden to the ancient maple that sits high on a hill in the yard, sheltering the house with its gracious canopy.

Alice has a wonderful life and she knows it. There's Tony, her college sweetheart of a husband, a philosophy major then, now pursuing an improbably successful career in the fashion industry. He commutes long hours and travels for weeks each year to provide this life for her and their two healthy, beautiful young daughters.

Last January they moved to this too-extravagant-for-her home on an acre of land, at the exurban rim of commutable distance to the big city, purchased so the girls could have a happy, carefree, old-fashioned childhood. Two nice cars. At least two vacations a year, one as a family, the other a getaway for just the two of them. Their own families live only an hour away. It all adds up to the American Dream, just as she had been taught to define it, all hers at the bright young age of twenty-nine.

Then why does she wake up every morning while it's still dark, to weep in the quiet of a household not yet stirring, while the sun cuts its swath toward morning? She doesn't know. All she knows is that in some deep, private place she feels empty and inexorably sad and, looking around at her beautiful life, she judges herself harshly for her feelings. What's more, there's no one to tell this to. Her mother? She'd only admonish her childishness and emotional self-indulgence. Her husband? He'd get exasperated and feel unappreciated for all his efforts. Friends and neighbors? Their afternoon child-surveillance-cum-chit-chat sessions are all about paint samples for the family room, or the baby's latest cute trick, or whether or not to become a classroom mother for Miss Idaveo's second grade. No, there is no one.

·· ♦ ··

And so Alice, not realizing it, experiences her First Saturn Return, the culmination of the Cycle of Preparation, hoping she can come to embrace and be thankful for what is, she wants to believe, the best time of her life.

DON AT 29

Sunday. Day of rest. Sleep in. Read the paper. Smell the coffee.

"Well, at least I can cover that last part," thinks Don as he slips out of bed carefully in the soft light of an early April morning so as not to wake up his wife. He makes his way past the closed bedroom doors of his three sleeping children to get to the tiny kitchen of the modest Cape Cod house that sits only blocks away from where he grew up.

The coffee maker has been set up the night before, and Don flips it on so it can brew his first cup while he goes over to the desk in the corner of the living room that serves as his entire home office. He gathers up the scrambled papers that hold this morning's sermon – his seminarian preaching debut – and puts them in order as he walks back to the kitchen. He pours a mug of coffee, splashes in some half-and-half, and settles in at the table.

"Not bad," he thinks to himself as he reads it over one last time, pen in hand, making only a few last-minute changes. "Not bad at all!"

Don has the life he dreamed of, and he knows it. And he sure worked overtime to achieve it. Starting from a childhood marred with violence and neglect, he was salvaged by the care and support of the minister of the only church within walking distance of the dilapidated building that was a house in name only and never a home. The refuge he found at church had saved and changed his life, providing not only an escape, but a destination. It was a place to go after school to shoot hoops and make friends; a place to make a contribution to something more than mere survival; a place to fall in love. It was there that he had found his sense of family, and became the virtual stepson who would carry the torch of a small-town ministerial dynasty into the next generation.

Don had fought hard for the right to make a life for himself. With the support of many, including the small scholarship that the minister's congregation had mustered for their "hometown boy," and huge dollop of simple good luck, he had made his way to this kitchen table, sermon in hand, congregation waiting – and wanting – to hear his preaching debut.

So why does he wake up in the middle of most nights feeling like he's being choked and can't breathe? He doesn't know. All he knows is that in some deep, private place he feels empty and inexorably sad, and looking around at his impossible-dream-come-true of a life, he judges himself harshly for his feelings. And who can he tell it to? His hard-working wife? She is holding things together with a part-time job and three small children while he spends every weekday in a seminary two states away, finishing up only his first year. How could he crush *her* piece of the dream? His mentor? After he had given so much and invoked congregational support? His family? Unthinkable. No, there is no one.

And so Don, not realizing it, experiences his First Saturn Return, the culmination of the Cycle of Preparation, hoping he can embrace and become once again truly thankful for what he expected would be just the beginning of a wonderful life.

THE CYCLE OF PREPARATION: SATURN

In *New Passages: Mapping Your Life Across Time,* Gail Sheehy observes that people are taking longer to grow up, that "true adulthood doesn't begin until thirty."[2] Astrology has known this for eons. You may indeed be living in accordance with all the conventional definitions of what constitutes adulthood well before age thirty: education completed; career underway; the responsibilities and joys of parenthood imminent, in place, or eliminated by choice; contributing to the society and community you live in…add what fits. However, from the astrological perspective, until you're about thirty years old, the preparation for the adult roles you have assumed is not finished because you simply haven't had enough time to complete the curriculum. Saturn, the Karmic Teacher, takes that long to finish teaching the course.

Saturn's lesson plan for our first twenty-nine years is a rigorous one, giving us the opportunity to learn what we need to learn, and experience what we need to experience in order to become fully qualified to assume the responsibilities and privileges of adulthood. Like the grading system for the Olympic diving competition, the assignments come with varying degrees of difficulty, but all will require focus, perseverance, and concentrated effort, because that's how Saturn gets things done.

During the Cycle of Preparation, the assignment that has the highest degree of difficulty is about getting to really know the person who is trying to pull off this adulthood thing. Without that knowledge, every other decision and plan may be up for grabs. In other words, there's no point in aspiring to become a quantum physicist if you can't stand math and won't even *try* to pull better than a D+ in algebra. So, during the period of learning and getting ready for adulthood, coming up with the right questions is at least as important as coming up with the right answers. Do we want to be a lawyer – or a movie actor – or continue the family tradition of excellence in generations of electricians? What about marriage and children? Do we want to live in the city or the country? Rent an apartment or own a home?

Once we develop a set of goals and dreams for ourselves, dreams that are in alignment with who we are and with what is achievable, we need to develop a game plan to actualize them, a plan that addresses issues like: What information,

---

SATURN STRATEGIES

Review the past. Evaluate the present. Plan for the future. Compare where you are now with where you thought you'd be.

Set short and long term goals. Make realistic, do-able plans to achieve them. Monitor progress.

Take an inventory of resources and skills relative to your goals. Fill in the gaps.

Be responsible. Pay attention to details.

Take a hard look at both tangible and energetic clutter. Clean it up.

Create something "earthy" and tangible. Plant something.

Be patient. Saturn work takes time.

competencies and resources do I need? Can I acquire them on my own or do I need help? What will it cost? What's my timeline? Is the plan realistic? Depending on the answer to these questions and our experience, we may need to tweak or even redefine our goals.

THE FIRST SATURN RETURN

The First Saturn Return is a time of serious evaluation of how well we have completed our preparation for adulthood. We look around and what we see is the product of what we thought we wanted, and what it has cost to get ourselves there. Perhaps the most important question to be answered at this time is: Are you going to continue on your current path, or look for other options?

Let's say you've made a real success of that big financial career you started after college. Is that growing pile of money as satisfying as you thought it would be? If not, why not? What *would* be? Maybe you thought that all you'd ever want was to be a stay-at-home mom, with a big house in a town with a great educational system, and enough leisure time to develop your tennis serve while the kids were at school. Is that still personally fulfilling enough for you? If not, what would fill the void? Or perhaps you've opted for the Peter Pan approach to life since leaving school: pick-up jobs to fund travel and good times, and a risky lifestyle with as little responsibility as possible. Are you starting to feel a little out of place with the twenty-year-olds you're hanging out with?

For many, major course corrections will be required at the First Saturn Return, and the degree of necessary change can be measured by how we're *feeling* about our lives at this time. So it may come as little or no surprise that Saturn, suited up for his equally important role of Authoritarian Parent, has not returned alone. About a year earlier, the sensitive, intuitive Moon arrived in *her* archetypal role of the Nurturing Parent. Yes, both Dad and Mom have returned to mark and celebrate this important rite of passage to adulthood.

———————— ☽ ————————

THE MOON

· · ◆ DESCRIPTION ◆ · ·

Represents: Emotions. Instinct and intuition. The unconscious. How we nurture and how we need to be nurtured ourselves. The part of us, regardless of gender, that is associated with female energy (the *anima*).

Negative Expression: Over-sensitivity. Emotional self-indulgence. Unconscious behavior that "runs the show" to our own or someone else's detriment.

Role: The Nurturing Parent. Mom.

The instinctual, sensitive, intuitive Moon represents our fundamental emotional make-up. By describing our inner, subjective selves, she helps us connect to our feelings and integrate that emotional intelligence into our consciousness. By describing the kind of nurturing we need, the Moon also helps us feel safe and secure in this world. Do you feel things deeply and take your emotions to heart, keeping them private in order to feel safe, or are you emotionally expansive, wearing your heart on your sleeve? Do you feel safe and loved when someone *tells* you how you make them smile the minute they see you, or do you need an arm around your shoulder and a big bear hug? The Moon's sign and placement in the birth chart give important insight into these dimensions.

In the world of astrological archetypes, the Moon represents Mom, the person who, regardless of actual gender, filled (or didn't) the need we all have to be cared for and loved unconditionally. The Moon can also tell a lot about whether or not we were likely to have *received* that nurturing and support when we were young, and how we will provide those qualities in all kinds of relationships throughout our lifetime.

THE PROGRESSED LUNAR CYCLE

In real time, the Moon makes its complete circuit of the birth chart in a little more than twenty-eight days, hardly an amount of time that can be considered to be of evolutionary importance. Knowing where the Moon is passing through your chart in "clock time" might help you decide whether to go on a weekend getaway or put your nose to the grindstone and clean out that cluttered garage, but the decision wouldn't be likely to impact your growth and development in any important way. Tracking the Moon's actual movement in clock time doesn't provide much insight into how we are evolving from the emotional, lunar perspective, simply because it moves too quickly.

Astrologers have figured out a mathematical formulation, called *progression,* that establishes a meaningful relationship between one *day* of the Moon's movement in real time and one *year* of our lives. Thus, during its *progressed lunar cycle*, the Moon takes about twenty-eight *years* to return to its natal position in the birth chart, moving at a tempo that allows us to observe the evolution of our emotional growth.

During almost three decades of progressed passage around the birth chart, the Moon spends about two and a half years in every sign, giving us the opportunity to experience what it's like to *feel* in accordance with qualities of each of those other eleven signs. For example, the natal Sagittarian Moon is an optimistic, outgoing, enthusiastic and adventurous Moon, as warm and friendly as a ten-week-old puppy. But it's not a particularly empathic Moon, and it is generally unaware that anyone might feel differently than itself, so it can be something of a well-meaning but insensitive Moon. Add the Sagittarian tendency to speak/act first, think later – and to "tell it like it is," often to a fault – and you can see that, as endearing and well-intended

MOON STRATEGIES

Spend quiet time alone in familiar, comfortable surroundings. Listen for the voice of your feelings.

Watch a movie or read a book that touches your heart. Browse through your children's baby pictures, or your own. Hug your pet, if you have one. How do you feel?

Stand out in the moonlight and soak it up.

Keep a journal. Record your emotional, intuitive reactions to life's experiences.

Trust your gut. Start with baby steps and build confidence.

Seek therapy to help understand yourself and to heal wounds.

Try to re-connect with family members if uncomfortable distance has developed.

as that natal Sagittarian Moon may be, it can also cause some serious problems with all kinds of relationships. However, the two and a half years spent progressing through the compassionate, sensitive, intuitive sign of Pisces, provides an opportunity to enrich its natal Sagittarian qualities with enhanced awareness of how others feel and react. And because the Moon also passes through each house of the birth chart during its twenty-eight year progressed cycle, it will spend significant time in the House of Partnership, where it will have the chance, through the give-and-take of relationship, to integrate qualities of compromise, negotiation, and diplomacy into its natal energetic palette. At the end of the progressed lunar cycle, that natal Sagittarian – or any sign – Moon can be deeper and richer emotionally, without having to give up any of the fine qualities of its basic nature.

THE CYCLE OF PREPARATION: THE MOON

Most of us can easily remember how we were feeling and how life was for us at our first Saturn Return, at around the age of twenty-nine. This is because shortly before that, the progressed Moon returned to its original position in the birth chart, spending a couple of months in close, intimate company with the natal Moon. The result is a period of doubled-up emotional self-awareness. Our life circumstances, and how we *feel* about them at this time, become strongly imprinted in our consciousness. And how we feel about our life will be commensurate with how successfully we have handled the fundamental lunar assignments during the Cycle of Preparation that is just ending. Once again, asking the right questions is at least as important as having the right answers:

1. *Have we developed emotional enrichment and maturity?* Are we in touch with our emotional nature and aware of our emotional reactions? Do we honor them or try to suppress them? Have we expanded our repertoire of emotional responses? Can we share our emotions with trustworthy people and create relationships of all kinds, based on appropriate levels of connection and mutual understanding? Do we understand that others may react and experience emotions differently from ourselves, and have we cultivated the awareness of how others are feeling?

2. *Have we become our own person without having to abandon where we come from?* Did we get what we needed in terms of nurturing, unconditional love and emotional support in our childhood? If not, were we able to find the help that would guide us to alternate resources of that security and support, including those within ourselves? Can we share those resources with others? Are we in touch with our roots and family of origin

> **The Planetary Playbook** that follows the **Epilogue** contains lots of practical information, suggestions, and strategies that can help you make the most of all the important astrological periods that occur in your lifetime.

as sources of love and support, but not blocked or confined by them? If not, have we come to terms with the situation and is there a plan to deal with it in a positive way?

These are big, important questions, and events in the biographical life at Saturn Return time may well reflect how they have been answered: an important reconciliation or reconnection; the birth of a child; the appearance of a physical symptom – a rash, a panic episode, a heaviness in the heart – that is found to have no underlying medical cause. The degree of happiness or upset will be commensurate with the grade on Mom's, *i.e.* the Moon's, contribution to the karmic report card.

• • ◆ • •

So there you have it – the culmination of the Cycle of Preparation, and the launch of the Cycle of Adulthood. The Moon has helped us do the inner work. Saturn has helped us manifest our growth – or lack of it – in the outer world. Is it any wonder why people *under* age thirty would think that anyone *over* age thirty doesn't "get them," and can't be trusted? It's popularly called the "Generation Gap." Astrologers call it "The First Saturn Return Gap."

The First Saturn Return can bring a sense of urgency to make things happen: to either expand and move forward into the existing direction of life, or to figure out why it isn't working and correct course. Will you take up the challenge or try to convince yourself it doesn't exist? This much I know: if *you* didn't take charge, the Universe will certainly step in.

Let's get back to Alice and Don.

ALICE'S AND DON'S KARMIC REPORT CARDS

Alice and Don are each surely living adult lives, fulfilling adult responsibilities. From any perspective, they've both accomplished a lot, and each is in a place that bears testimony to their hard work. But at this time of cycles ending and beginning, Alice and Don, unknown to one another, share feelings of emptiness and incomprehensible sadness. A look back over the years that have led them to this moment will provide some insight.

ALICE'S FIRST SATURN RETURN REPORT CARD

There's no question that, at age twenty-nine, Alice has hit the American Dream Jackpot: the upscale home; the perfect family; a husband streaking along the corporate fast-track; two terrific kids; two cars in the garage; even a couple of dogs. It's what she's been taught to aspire to and trained to achieve, and good girl that she is, she worked hard to Ace every assignment along the way.

She comfortably stretched her intellect and uncomfortably stretched her awkward athletic and social skills to create the high school record that would assure admittance to any college or university that her first-generation parents could financially support. Then, she delivered on that action point by graduating with honors, Phi Beta Kappa key in hand. Two months later, she walked down the aisle to Tony, although if she could have been honest with herself, she would have admitted to envy of her college roommate who, instead of starting a teaching career that fall like Alice, would be heading off for a year in Europe with her best friend from high school. Alice, instead, had followed the familial and societal script, even to the point of becoming a teacher or nurse, something she could "easily go back to" after she raised her still-to-be-born children.

In other words, "Adult" Alice had given more thought to her wedding plans than to the trajectory of her own life, and was already faintly starting to suspect that the independence and excitement of her college years might turn out to have been the best years of her life.

The Moon interjects here with her contribution to the First

Saturn Return report card. What about Alice's emotional maturity and enrichment? Has she been able to become her own person without abandoning where she came from?

Well, Alice certainly *feels* her life. She fell hard for Tony, the charming, popular, athletic big man on campus. She followed her heart on that count, even against major resistance based on her family's evaluation of Tony's ability to deliver on the "successful-on-the-way-up" prerequisite, and embarrassing-to-Alice social discrimination issues involving his ethnicity and familial social status. Was defiance and escape mixed in with her decision to marry so quickly after college? Of course, though at the time she could not see it. What she does occasionally glimpse at age twenty-nine is how she has over-compensated by allowing an unhealthy level of familial interference intrude on her marriage.

Yes, she's an excellent, loving mother who is committed to doing nothing but the best for her daughters. But what is she doing to nurture *herself*? And what about the voice of her heart, stirring the tears that are falling into her morning coffee? Why is she so clueless as to their source?

Saturn steps in with the meat and potatoes perspective, and from that point of view Alice is largely on solid ground. She's responsible, effective, hard-working, determined, and efficient in support of her husband and family's needs. She's even taken up tennis and rekindled her college expertise in bridge to enhance their social options as a couple. But does she even have any goals of her own – for herself alone? For that matter, does she even realize that she's entitled to them?

Alice's life looks so good on the outside. She's accomplished a lot. She's "living the dream." But it's not *her* dream because she doesn't even realize that she can – and should – have one for herself. And if she even got as far as to want a dream, what could it be if she doesn't even know who she is?

At best, Alice is barely pulling a C+.

Don's First Saturn Return Report Card

At age twenty-nine Don has virtually reinvented himself, and the odds against him being able to pull it off had been monumental. He had started out from as close to Ground Zero as a person can be.

His childhood had been lived in financial and emotional poverty occasioned by his violent father's abdication of bread-winner responsibilities by the age of forty, and his mother's literal-by-death abdication of her ineffectual and beaten-back life by the age of fifty-six. Don and his three siblings had pretty much raised themselves on their own. The church and its people were a life-line for all of them, but especially for Don, who came to build his own life around that base of support and direction. Who could question the strategy? What other options were there?

The Moon observes that, from her perspective, in many ways Don has done the best he could with what he had. He learned not to let violence and emotional neglect immobilize and destroy him, although the Universal Nurturing Parent suspects that in order to pull it off, he has largely unplugged himself from his own feelings. Still, he gets high marks for trusting his internal guidance system in order to take care of himself and survive. As to whether or not he's been able to become his own person without abandoning where he came from, that's a complex issue. Certainly distance was the prerequisite for survival, but has he switched family allegiance, only to create an emotional dependency that could compromise his own selfhood and wholeness? It may be too early to tell.

Saturn's evaluation is a lot more certain, in large part because his realm is not fraught with nuance. Don has not only survived, but has found positive substitutes for the parental and familial influences that were absent in his own family of origin. He is pedaling as fast as he can to learn quickly, catch up, and move forward. He's identified with the path of his surrogate father, and mustered the discipline and resourcefulness to get the education and experience he needs in order to prepare himself for the ministry. And he's received enough nurturing and support from his mentor's family and congregation to risk establishing a marriage and family of his own.

It's taken a lot of his energy and focus to get this new venture off to the right start, so it's been easy to brush off some early-warning signs of things getting shaky at home. Baby Laurie's unplanned arrival so shortly after second child Christine's had opened the door to a version of the chaos and confusion that colored his own childhood. Don has allowed himself to believe that what was happening belonged to Jean's stay-at-home mom's domain, and not only did he not want to undermine her authority and status there, he feels that his seminary work requires his full attention, especially in this first year.

Saturn likes that Don is responsible to his goals and commitments, and, to the extent that he has been able, has given his life to a dream that is his own, even though Don might be starting to suspect that it could be flawed. Don doesn't know what he doesn't know. Those middle-of-the-night moments of fear and sadness are a big clue, but right now his focus is to quell his concerns and keep moving forward. And what's he going to do about the home front? For now, he'll probably just get even busier to keep his mind off his doubts and concerns.

Don had a really rough row to hoe, and he's come so far. Saturn awards a solid B. For now.

But it's not a competition. The Karmic Teacher's report card evaluates each person only against themselves and their own potential, so the only question that matters is "Where does each of them go from here?"

ENTR'ACTE: MY CHILD, THE POSTER CHILD – SASHA, AGE 28

Sasha alit like a hummingbird to hover for a quick visit home between trips to far-flung corners of the world where she worked on women's health care and infant mortality initiatives with the governments and agencies of emerging nations. By any standard she was living an exciting, meaningful life, although the path to it had followed anything but a straight trajectory.

She had majored – and excelled – in mathematics in college because she "liked it," but not enough to teach or pursue the required graduate degrees for research and scientific work. She tried accounting and couldn't stand it for being "too boring and dull," a death sentence totally in alignment with her curious, quick Gemini nature. On to a Master's Degree in Urban Planning, first at the "inadequate program" at the *first* eminent university, moving on to the "right program" at the *second* eminent university where she received the degree. During an internship at a quasi-governmental agency, she discovered the work she believed was her true calling – interesting, stimulating, challenging, and, most of all, making a difference. In recent years, she had often travelled her world-wide way in the company of Stephen, who was, after a long list of "Big Almosts," to become the "Keeper."

By all objective measures, Sasha had arrived at her first Saturn Return on target for the A+ in life that she had always striven for academically.

"Mom, could you get out your tarot cards? I want to check something out."

"Sure."

It was a beautiful late spring day, so I spread the special purple velvet cloth out over the table in a shady, breeze-free corner of the garden, and began the ritual.

"Shuffle the cards while you silently think of the question, Sash. Don't tell it to me until you've finished and handed back the cards. You want to focus the energy."

I rolled the chambered nautilus shell that always seemed to help release the cards' messages between my hands while she shuffled and then returned the deck.

"OK. What's the question?"

"Will I be going to medical school?"

"Huh???!!" With an involuntary small shake of my head, I paused and set the deck on the table.

"I'll explain, Mom...just read the cards. Please."

Sure enough, there it was, prominent in the layout: The Death Card – the old world was giving way to something new. Contrary to popular understanding of the card as ominous, it signifies that something promising and hopeful is growing out of seeds and situations that might have been meaningful in the past, but are no longer relevant to the future. Although she might not have put it exactly in these terms, Sasha's intellect, and experiences, and intuition, along with an openness to act on the insights from that combination, had led her to recognize that life – as good as it was – was not all that it could or should be during the cycle that was on the verge of launching.

Here's what happened over the next several years. She

- completed an intensified, one-year bachelor-level program of pre-med science courses and got a great score on the MCATs;

- married Stephen and moved to New England to establish residency so she could pay in-state costs at the state university medical school if she got accepted (which she did);

- applied for and was awarded government grants that paid

for three of the med school years in exchange for a commitment to devote the first three years of her practice to the
medically underserved (which was, to her, the whole point
of the shift anyhow, of course);

- gave birth to their daughter, my darling granddaughter
  Lulu, in her senior year and *still* graduated first in her class
  (that is, if the school had had a policy of acknowledging
  that status);

- completed her residency and moved to Texas to serve her
  three-year commitment, staying on after it was fulfilled.

By the time of the first Saturn checkpoint, about seven years
after the Saturn Return, with focused intent, a willingness to risk
following her inner knowing, and a monumental amount of hard
work, Sasha had re-invented her life, bringing it into a quite stun-
ning alignment with who she is and what she values.

The ups and downs and the work of growing and becoming continue for Sasha, as it does for all of us. It is my great blessing to be
her mother and to get to witness it.

CHAPTER 4

HALFTIME: THE MIDLIFE TRANSITS

(AGES 40-44)

"Midlife is when you reach the top of the ladder, only to find out that it was leaning against the wrong wall."

JOSEPH CAMPBELL

THE WHISTLE BLOWS LOUD AND CLEAR FOR THE HALFTIME BREAK. THE team heads to the locker room to regroup, recoup, and reorient themselves to the game as it's been played thus far. They strategize for the second half. Psychologists and sociologists call this time of life the Midlife Crisis. Astrology takes a more neutral stance, referring to the energy passages that move through everyone's chart between the ages of approximately 40-44 as the *Midlife Transits.*

The timing is nothing short of exquisite. Although the body may be starting to softly whisper at future vulnerabilities, energies are high and life stretches out seemingly endlessly into the future.

Consider one end of the spectrum, someone at the top of their game, doing just what they have hoped and planned to do, just what they are "supposed" to do. Life is running at full throttle. Job/career, family, recreation, sociability, perhaps even some spiritual and/or social consciousness and involvement are all in the mix, juggled and re-juggled in what can sometimes feel like the caucus race in *Alice in Wonderland.* The caucus race is run by the Dodo, who sets up a "sort of a circle" race course. Everyone starts running when they like, and stops when they like, so that, to the observer *or the* participant, it's impossible to know when the race begins or ends, or whether or not anyone wins. Life at halftime can feel just like that. Still, it seems rich with opportunity and importance, pleasure and satisfaction, and there's a feeling of control over one's destiny.

Then there's the other extreme. Imagine the person who never finished the work of preparing for adulthood and isn't worrying much about playing catch-up, either. Perhaps the body isn't as fit and energetic as it could be, thanks to neglect, excess, or some combination of both. A succession of short-lived, dead-end jobs has culminated in an ever-diminishing number of remaining unemployment checks and slim prospects for a new position. Failed relationships (if they could even be called that) of all kinds litter the pathways of memory. The person is alone. Uncertain. Maybe even scared.

Most of us enter our forties somewhere in the middle, skewed toward the positive end of the spectrum. But no matter where *we* are in the continuum, the planets have been making their way through the zodiac, and through our energy fields. **As in so much of life, it's not what happens to us that's important, it's what we *do* with what happens to us that counts.** Paradoxically, success by personal and societal standards at this time of life can be something of a disadvantage, making it hard to even think of slowing down long enough to take in – never mind evaluate – where we are and where we want to get to. After all, there are no referees' whistles to stop the clock on *this* game.

Or are there...?

Let's check in with Alice and Don.

ALICE AT 44

Alice's eyes pop open and check the clock radio on the night stand. As always, it reads 5:48AM, exactly two minutes before the alarm is set to go off. Waiting only long enough for the right-hand number to switch from 8 to 9, she hits the "Off" button, jumps out of bed, tugs briefly at the quilt, pulling it haphazardly over the crumpled sheets, and heads for the shower. Toby sleepily emerges from his currently favorite hidey-hole in the back of her closet, blinks open his bleary blue eyes, and greets her with a swish of tail against her leg. He pays his respects to the litter box and resettles himself in the still-warm tangle of bedcovers.

With military precision, Alice is out of the shower and dry after five minutes, smoothly sliding into the rest of her morning routine. Downstairs in the kitchen, the coffee has already started to brew and by 6:20AM, she is dressed and has already given the first human wake-up call to her perennially sleepy-headed adolescent daughters. She heads downstairs and pours her first cup of coffee as she sets out the juice, cereal, and milk for her girls.

A half hour later Alice is in her office, only three short miles away. She turns on her computer and, as it boots up, calls home to be sure that Sasha and Nikki are awake and on schedule for the 7:45 school bus.

Just another day in Paradise, but for Alice, this *is* Paradise and she knows it. Over the past five years she has worked hard to define it and to develop a plan to get herself there.

Her journals, bed-written in the still, dark moments before sleep, not only document the journey, but saved her sense of self while the world as she knew it disintegrated and then lay in ruins.

First, the dissolution of the "perfect" marriage, complete with all the standard *accoutrements*: deceptions, accusations, denials, embarrassment, and contrite, short-lived multiple reconciliations. The whole dreary, heart-breaking, confidence-eroding, fear-invoking, stereotypical, made-for-television-movie-unless-its-*your*-marriage process took more than a few years to finalize.

Then, the scribbled, ever-shortening entries of the next three years, entries that document the fast-track turnaround that was sustained at times only by her love and concern for the girls, and her growing commitment to her own life:

- Going back to school to learn computers so that she could

have a real, self-supporting career, and then the huge sense of relief and pride when, after landing a great job, she was able to tell Tony to cut back on the alimony. Everyone thought she was nuts, especially her happy Ex. Only *she* knew she was anything but.

• Moving from the house that was never really *her* home, to a smaller, more manageable, far more loveable place in the same town, so the girls could have one less disruption in their already-disrupted lives. It was a move that feathered their college fund nests in the bargain.

• Moving out – albeit with baby, baby steps – into a social world that was more in alignment with her newly-minted single status. In fact, a journal entry only last week mentioned a good-looking guy at the Unitarian singles group that seemed awfully interesting and sweet in a goofy-cute way...but no, she's not ready for that part yet!

Catching herself drifting off into an early morning daydream, Alice lingers only a moment more in her trip down memory lane, long enough only to reflect how, if Tony hadn't left, she might have still been helplessly and cluelessly crying into her pre-dawn coffee. *"There's a lot that's too hectic, and too scary, and too lonely about life these days, but it's my life – and getting more my own every day. I wouldn't want it any other way,"* she thinks, repeating the mantra that helps her feel safe.

Alice writes herself a reminder to pick up some take-out for the girls' supper. She's giving herself a night out with a friend from work, going to an astrology lecture at the local community college. With that done, she heads down to the cafeteria for the morning's last cup of coffee (hold the tears).

••◆••

Back at her desk, Alice removes the lid from the coffee cup and gingerly takes a sip. She digs into her purse, retrieves a pack of cigarettes, lights up, and happily begins to untangle a particularly irksome piece of computer code, not thinking any longer about how far she's come, but never forgetting it for a minute.

DON AT 44

Don opens his eyes abruptly and checks his watch. 6:45AM. Perfect. Good thing he never has needed an alarm clock – there's not even one spare nickel kicking around these days. Not with the alimony and child support payments for the girls, plus the costs of raising his son – and keeping the car on the road, and paying the rent on this bargain-basement, off-season, not exactly warm-enough beach rental. *Where will we go for the summer? It's only February, no time to think about it now – something will work out.* All this, juggled on a teacher's salary that's still on one of the lowest rungs of the pay scale, plus the proceeds from the three-night-a-week bread truck delivery job and occasional after-school tutoring sessions.

The past few years have been rough, no question about it, and it isn't going to get smoother any time soon. But the big moves have been made. It almost even feels right, and something inside tells him that it *is* right. The night terrors are all but gone. In the past few years Don has gotten his teaching degree, found a job, and earned his tenure status. And, after an earnest but futile attempt at reconciliation, he had finally left the marriage that had spiraled out of control after his irrevocable decision to leave seminary after the first year.

Shattering Jean's dream of being the Minister's Wife had been the last straw for a relationship that had started to deteriorate almost from the moment their first child was born, just less than a year after their marriage. Bobby had not been an easy baby – high-energy, little need for sleep, colicky – and Christine's arrival less than eighteen months later, followed by Laurie's less than two years after *that*, had sent them into a nightmare of confusion, anger, and unbridled chaos. The situation had stirred memories of his own childhood, and the combination had rendered him virtually powerless to bring peace and stability to the domestic war zone. At the end of the day, there was nothing to do but to leave – with his books, his clothes, and the family's second-hand dilapidated second car, the one that was only ever meant to be used for grocery store runs, and never for what was now his thirty-mile commute to work. And, most importantly, he had left with Bobby.

Don gets out of bed and heads for the bathroom, stopping first in the living room where his son sleeps on the pull-out couch. He stoops to shake Bobby's shoulder gently for a first wake-up call, and continues on his way, anticipating the upcoming struggle to get him fed and dressed so they both can arrive at school on time.

"What would I have done if they hadn't let him enroll in my school district?" he muses, and then pushes the thought aside as a waste of energy. Best to think about the logistics of the complicated day that is dawning. There's the after-school meeting with the Child Study Team to discuss his son's behavioral issues in class. Then I have to drop him off at my sister's, where he'll spend the night while I do the mid-week bread truck run. I have to complete next week's lesson plan during my free period so I can get it to the Department Chairman on time. And how can I fit in the nap I need if I'm going to stay awake at the wheel of the bread truck and not get lost in the dark of those wind-y, confusing back roads between towns?

It's not like tomorrow will be any easier. I'll have to wake up a half hour earlier to pick Bobby up on the way back to school and, after the staff meeting, it's our night to have supper with Christine and Laurie at the diner. And Good God – I forgot! It's their weekend with us starting on Saturday. I have to stop by sometime at Mike's and pick up the cots.

No time for coffee – not even instant. He heads back to the living room and shakes his 10-year-old's shoulder less gently than before, standing at his bedside until Bobby's feet hit the floor.

All in a day's work – in a life's day for Don. No time to think about how far he's come, or even where he's heading...for now, anyway. For now, it's one foot in front of the other, step after step into the future, sustained by the unquenched confidence, if he had even a minute to think of it, that it will only get better.

He turns back to pull Bobby out of bed and wrangle him through the morning routine.

The degree of crisis, chaos, and frenetic activity at the midlife can be a barometer of the degree of disconnect between the authenticity of who we are and the biographical life we have been living. It can be a time of confusion as the realization dawns that, being human, we can't control everything; that we may have to make new, hard choices based on the outcome of old decisions and commitments or, at a minimum, deal with the consequences of choices that we have made. Some tighten the yoke and settle, plodding forward, already feeling somehow gray and sad and washed out, not even realizing that they may be choosing a path that leads to a life half-lived. Others will keep the plates spinning, denying the passage. They focus on familiar goals – the next great-but-same career success, having a menopause baby – trying to sustain the illusion of youth, not realizing that repeating the past is *not* forward motion. Still others will "walk off the job": the middle manager turned garage-band guitarist; the mid-life spouse leaving abruptly for a much-younger new lover. And some – the lucky ones – will slow down long enough to heed the call of that soft inner voice, the one asking "Is this all there is?" "What does it all mean?"

At its best, halftime can be a hugely creative period, the passage to a whole or at least partial new beginning, a time when, within the context of legitimate limitations and responsibilities, we can correct our mistakes, set new or revised goals, and claim new energies and abilities that can be used to move towards those objectives. In so doing, we can strengthen the foundations for the time when we can "meaningfully return to ourselves" at the Second Saturn

Return, without having to grieve for the unlived potential of the time that has gone before.

But we are not alone. We need only look to the left and the right. Every seat in the boat is taken by one of our cohorts, people of our own generation, and the midlife transits are flowing through each of us. What's more, the Universe, as always, stands ready with limitless guidance, encouragement, and support, if only we can recognize it and claim it. Moving in their timeless, eternal pathways through the zodiac, three important planets will make contact with their natal positions in our birth charts as we transit the ages of 40-44: Uranus, Neptune, and, of course, Saturn. Each will seek our attention in its own unique way and remind us of the resources and support it offers. Each asks important questions to stir awareness, consciousness, and resolve. Each urges us to grow and evolve in the direction of releasing the unique and altogether wonderful energies and potential of our own selves and birth charts.

··◆··

We start with Uranus, who arrives first, typically when we are between the ages of 40-42.

URANUS

· · ◆ DESCRIPTION ◆ · ·

Represents: Uniqueness and individuality. Authenticity. Brilliance. Spontaneity. Sudden, unforeseen change.

Negative Expression: Extreme eccentricity. Insensitivity. Touchiness. Disruption.

Role: Auntie Mame. The Wizard. Albert Einstein.

I like to think of Sammy Davis, Jr. as the Uranian poster child. By his own description, he was a one-eyed, black, short, Jewish guy, married (at the time) to a tall, blonde, gorgeous Scandinavian actress; a man whose personal anthem was "I gotta be me!" and who lived by that credo until his very last breath.

The planet Uranus was first discovered at the end of the 18th century during the times of the American and French Revolutions, times when history-changing battles were fought in the name of an individual's rights to freedom and independence. It was a synchronous, meaningful discovery, and so not at all unusual in the world of astrology. Uranus is a planetary wizard, a great awakener who charges our energy field with the magic and excitement of the unexpected, and the thrill of opportunity and change. It asks us to claim our inalienable right to be our authentic selves, and to celebrate that individuality. Uranus calls us to live according to our own inner light at the highest, most evolved level we can pull off, discarding what is false in ourselves without succumbing to irresponsibility, mindless rebellion, or self-isolating eccentricity. And it insists that we walk this path in a way that doesn't impinge on anyone *else's* right to the very same things.

Like the rest of its planetary allies, Uranus always operates for our highest good, so in the service of its mandate, it offers help. Uranian kind of help. Its energy is bright, spontaneous, and sudden. It delivers its best messages by speaking to the genius in all of us, through ideas that come ahead of their time, out of the blue, and out of the box, like the shortcut from Point A to Point B that works in direct defiance of the judgmental voice of the societal and/or familial GPS. Uranus speaks to us through breakthroughs and sudden awakenings in the part of us that feels alive and excited about life and its possibilities. It reminds us not to get stuck in a rut; to look to the future; to be ourselves.

Is Uranus at work always comfortable? In some way all of us tend toward stability and security, even those Type A personalities who live in the energetic equivalent of the Indianapolis 500. How do you think *they* would react if their driver's license was suspended for six months and they had to use public transportation to get where they needed to go? It would be probably just as upsetting as if I had to take their place in the racecar driver's seat.

THE URANUS CYCLE

Uranus takes approximately eighty-four years to buzz its way around the birth chart, spending about seven years in each of the twelve signs and houses. Its circuit defines the astrological **Cycle of Individuation**, a life-long period of opportunity to recognize and develop our authenticity, and to gain freedom from what limits the expression of our own true selves.

Every twenty-one years during this cycle, Uranus makes important energetic connections to where it sits in its unchanging natal position in our birth chart. These are times when life's rhythms accelerate, times of awakening, times when any disconnect between your own true self and the outside self you inhabit in order to make your way in the world becomes intolerable, and as demanding of your attention as a two-year-old wanting his lost binky. In these Uranian times we are asked to risk change so that we're not left with a life that is somehow wrong for us, one in which we become a false self, a ghost who has floated away from anything resembling our own reality.

Times when Uranus is active in our charts are periods of intense improvisation, times when we're experimenting with new ways of being in our lives: a sudden job transfer to a foreign country; the twenty-five year old son who has to move back home because he can't find work after getting his masters degree; the deal falling through on the sale of your home just before you're getting ready to move to a new one. Everything becomes subject to revision. We have to be open to change and to letting go of the obsolete. We need to be flexible, as light on our metaphorical energetic platform as a boxer is on his feet. We are being challenged to re-invent ourselves, and the jackpot promise of the freedom and confidence that comes out of being able to be who we really are is worth whatever effort it takes. In the accelerated pace of the Uranian "buzz," we need to be careful not to let restlessness and impulsiveness lead us to self-defeating behavior: rebelliousness, change for the sake of change, or rash, ill-considered action. On the other

---

URANUS STRATEGIES

Risk change: you're ready for it. Anyway, you're simply not powerful enough to stop it. Bless necessary losses and let them go. Make room for what's coming in.

Do something "out of the box."

Trust the gut, but use the noggin. Uranus' bright ideas come suddenly, out of the blue. Run them through Saturn's feasibility radar.

Watch fireworks.

Expect resistance.

Pace yourself. Don't go overboard.

Stay connected. Get feedback.

Do a good deed in a big way.

---

hand, if a decision is in order, it's always best to make it ourselves, or Uranus might have to make it for us.

During Uranian times, relationship fireworks of all kinds are a definite possibility. People who have grown comfortable with the status quo may not applaud and welcome every baby or giant step we take on the path to our own authenticity, and the closer the relationship, the bigger the potential for seismic reactions. If a relationship ends, it's a sign that paths are diverging, not that it was necessarily in any way a mistake. Space is being made for each person to grow in new directions. New relationships, more in alignment with who we are becoming, are right in the wings, waiting for their cue. If, however, a relationship endures, it will be marked by new freedom and authenticity for each person involved.

Is it any wonder that Uranian transits can be unsettling, and fraught with sudden, unusual, and unexpected events?

When Uranus pays its call in our early forties, the success of its passage is measured by whether or not we engage in its energies and opportunities without going overboard. Did we step up to the plate and make ourselves open to the idea of change, or did we try to bury awareness and ignore the signals? Did we stand up for our own individuality and authenticity without abdicating our responsibilities, unnecessarily jeopardizing important relationships, or intruding on others' rights to their own lives? Did we push the envelope so far that we isolated ourselves in our own alien terrain, without a bridge to connect back to the world we live in? The answers to these questions feed straight to the mid-term report card.

·◆·◆·◆·

The planet Neptune joins the midlife gathering towards the end of the Uranian visitation. With all the buzz and action that's been going on, it helps to consciously anticipate her arrival, because her voice is very soft.

NEPTUNE

· · ◆ DESCRIPTION ◆ · ·

Represents: Spirituality. Direct contact with the Divine. Dreams. Creativity. Intuition. Imagination. Vision.

Negative Expression: Confusion. Apathy. Deception. Denial. Escapism. Addiction.

Role: The Monk or Nun. The Artist. The Visionary.

Watery, sensitive, spiritual Neptune, swathed in clouds of dreams and imagination, represents the part of each of us that seeks higher levels of consciousness and inspiration. Her place in our natal chart describes how and where we can best make direct contact with the timeless Universal energy and wisdom that underlies the physical, material life we're living here on Planet Earth.

Unlike her outgoing, even raucous, fellow traveler Uranus, Neptune's style is soft and her manner quite subtle. Still, her ways are seductive and get our attention all the same. Neptune is absolutely *not* logical, and anything but materialistic and practical, and she calls us not to action, but to reflection and solitude. Neptune smudges the boundaries of ego. She thins the veil between ourselves and Spirit so that the Universe can speak to us from the deep, intuitive place inside us where the vastness of our inner world is linked to the vastness of the Universe and its wisdom. It's best to intentionally create an environment that invites Neptune's presence, one where the cell phone has been powered down and the ringer turned off on the land line; one where the kids are out on a play date and, with no chance of interruption, you can sink softly into the comforts of a favorite easy chair, close your eyes, and relax – or break out the watercolors and work on the painting you started two years ago. Setting the stage sends the message to the Universe that we're engaged in the moment and process at hand, and it's definitely the way to go. But if we don't get around to it, Neptune has her own ways to slow us down and get our attention: sadness, apathy, inertia, even illness and escapist addiction, if necessary.

Neptune also represents the unconscious, that part of ourselves which, by definition, we don't know much about. The unconscious is the repository of unrecognized gifts and talents and abilities. But it also holds memories and parts of ourselves, real or imagined, that can be painful to confront – unrecognized obstacles and impediments to our own forward motion. It is also where the connection between our body, mind, and spirit is made, which is why Neptune is one of the planets associated with wholeness and healing. It should come as little or no surprise that therapy of all kinds is one of Neptune's most powerful tools. So is creativity, because Neptune is all about inspiration – literally, the "drawing in of Spirit." Neptune helps us build consciousness, heal wounds, claim strengths and abilities that we didn't even know we had, and create a vision for our future.

Like all planets, Neptune's energy is neutral, and how it operates in our life and world correlates to how we use our free will and choice to manifest it. So, we need to look at some of Neptune's low-end manifestations in order to spot them if and when they show up.

For starters, the very sensitivities that facilitate consciousness and inspiration can resemble a fog attack, leading us down a soft-ly-sloping, *un*conscious path to a whole laundry list of delusory and illusory self-defeating dead ends: escapism, apathy, depression, debilitation, "why me?" consciousness, self-pity...the list seems endless. At this low end, Neptune can be an energy vampire, seductively sneaking up on us and draining us of clarity and initiative and optimism. It can amp up our sensitivities to our own and others' pain to the point where we become the walking (or loung-ing-around) wounded: too weakened to act; too confused to be objective; lost in a self-created or chemically-induced, overly-comfortable, apathetic drift.

It's up to each of us to recognize the signs of when "taking five" becomes, instead, inertia; when sensitivity starts our hearts to bleed and bleed until they are sucked dry; when whatever it is that we're doing is putting distance between ourselves and what it *really* takes to heal the wound, solve the problem, write the poem, get the job done, or make the true connection to ourselves and to Spirit. Early intervention is important. One of Neptune's most precious treasures, the ability to thin the boundaries between body, mind, and spirit, makes it possible for each of us to take the lead in integrating that trinity positively into our own energy fields. But we don't want to trigger that body-mind connection in a negative way, literally making ourselves sick.

THE NEPTUNE CYCLE

Neptune takes about 165 years to drift through the twelve signs and houses of the birth chart, so barring unforeseen and unforeseeable-at-this-time quantum leaps in geriatric research, no one experiences a Neptune return. However, in the course of our lifetimes, it will make contact with all the planets in our birth chart, including important connections to itself in its own natal position. Neptune transits are times when we become sensitized to our own and others' energies. Intuition and our ability to tap into our own inner lives and visualize the future's possibilities are at a peak, so although it can be hard to reconnect with our cerebral life lines, we don't want to miss catching the Neptunian wave. Staying awake and aware can assure that we leverage Neptune's opportunities without falling into its seductive, loss-of-self whirlpools.

One quarter of its way through its cycle, around the age of forty-one or forty-two, the oceanic planet makes what is arguably this lifetime's most significant aspect to its natal self, and it could not have picked a better time. The scramble to deliver on adult responsibilities and important goals is running at full tilt, and without some celestial intervention, life is at risk of depletion and exhaustion in pursuit of goals that may no longer be viable, or even desirable. At a minimum, those goals and the strategies to achieve them are in need of examination, and perhaps retooling. And it goes without saying that, in the midlife mayhem, the chances of having the time and being able to connect to one's own inner core can be at an all-time low.

Enter the Neptune drift: vague confusion; malaise and discontent; a sense of depletion and vulnerability; perhaps a sadness that stands quietly to the side, waiting to be acknowledged. "Is this all there is?" "Where is the excitement and expectation of what feels like only moments ago?" "Why am I tired...and unsure of myself?" "What's going on?" This is why it's not unusual for a person's first serious engagement with the therapeutic process to happen now.

Make no mistake: Neptune is playing a very important role in the halftime "show." We *need* to slow down, and soften the edges

NEPTUNE STRATEGIES

Slow down. Spend time in soothing, calm spaces, or in nature, near water. Do yoga. Meditate. Pray.

Envision your future. Dream a big dream.

Keep a dream journal. Look for repeated themes and symbols.

Do something creative. Don't worry about what you produce.

Grieve losses and pain. Then move on, focusing on new opportunities.

Seek therapy to discover what you don't know about yourself.

Be patient with the "Neptune Fog." Clarity *will* emerge. Still, don't get lost in the drift. **Do not** make big decisions until the passage is over. Wait for the clarity.

Let yourself feel tired.

Do something charitable and compassionate.

of our own certainty with Neptune's clouds of sensitivity and vagueness: to slow down so we can listen to our feelings and get in touch with the wisdom and guidance of our infallible, internal GPSs; to slow down so we can learn that there may be something beyond the world of the here and now that we need and want to connect to. The degree of confusion and discouragement, and the level of inertia, will be commensurate with the amount of slow-down required to get you to do that work of "re-*vision*ing" your own life.

Neptune is also the planet of dreams. At midlife, it asks us to dream BIG; to dissolve the boundaries of what we believed to be possible; to envision an integrated ideal for our lives, one that encompasses both internal consciousness and connection with external accomplishment, and incorporates Uranus' call for authenticity. It's not Neptune's job to consider the practicalities of the dream. Saturn will come along shortly and do the feasibility study.

You need to hang tough: clarity and direction *will* emerge. The Universe guarantees it if you stay the course. Because Neptune does its best work below the surface-tension of our outer world, you need to spend time quietly and alone to hear its messages, and the insights and gifts of its contributions may take a while to manifest in the outer life. **Neptune requires patience...and surrender... and trust.** In other words, it requires living in the unknown and unsure, and making no big, irreversible decisions. During this time, while its energies are active, the opportunity to mistake the extra glass or two – or three – of cabernet, or a loss of self in some other kind of escapist behavior, for an experience of spiritual enlightenment is at an all-time high. It's important to work on being able to loosen up enough to dream the big dream without jumping off the Acapulco cliff at a low tide of escapism and self-delusion.

Of course, how we handle Neptune's passage goes straight to the bottom line. *i.e.* Saturn's mid-term report card.

——————— ♄ ———————

SATURN

Somewhere around the age of forty-four, Saturn is at the halfway point of its twenty-nine-year methodical circuit around the birth chart. It stands exactly 180° opposite its own natal position, thereby announcing that it's time for the mid-term exams and report card. Uranus and Neptune have preceded him, and the results of their passages will, of course, contribute to the evaluation. (**NOTE:** To personalize the midlife experience, check your *Compass* bookmark for the second Saturn checkpoint period.)

True to character, Saturn wants us to "get real." It's not like he denies or wants to override his fellow planets' contributions and perspectives. Quite the contrary. It's simply that Saturn's job is to make it all happen in the world of the here and now, and that takes what *he* does best: analysis, goal-setting, planning, organization, and so forth.

The first order of business is to check back to the First Saturn Return. How does life line up now with how it was then? Have we accomplished what we set out

> ## SATURN STRATEGIES
>
> Review the past. Evaluate the present. Plan for the future. Compare where you are now with where you thought you'd be.
>
> Set short and long term goals. Make realistic, do-able plans to achieve them. Monitor progress.
>
> Take an inventory of resources and skills relative to your goals. Fill in the gaps.
>
> Be responsible. Pay attention to details.
>
> Take a hard look at both tangible and energetic clutter. Clean it up.
>
> Create something "earthy" and tangible. Plant something.
>
> Be patient. Saturn work takes time.

to do? Were we true to our responsibilities? Were we accountable for our actions? Did we act with integrity? Are the goals we set back then still valid, or has the experience of the intervening years changed them? If so, how? Are the revamped goals realistic?

Next, Saturn asks us to develop the tactical plan. How are we going to get from Point A to Point B? Is there any catch-up or patch-up to be done before we can begin? Do we need to acquire new skills and/or information? What changes, if any, must be made to the life we're living? What will it cost? What's the timeline?

Finally, the focus shifts to looking through the spy glass into the future, down the road fourteen or fifteen years to the Second Saturn Return. For now, it's a high-level assessment: How do we want life to look when we're launching the next cycle? Is there anything to consider in our plans now to put ourselves on course for *that* time? Admittedly, it's hard to even conceive of our sixties when we're at the energetic apex of our forties, but if we can muster the willingness to do it, we can subtly orient ourselves in that direction going forward, much in the way that we unconsciously adjust our trajectory for the most direct route to a certain point by simply identifying the target destination.

One thing's for certain: If we're not pulling at least a B, Saturn is going to have to dish up a pretty heavy-handed "heads up" in the down-to-earth world of our everyday life to get our attention and try to get us back on track.

> **Reminder: The Planetary Playbook** that follows the **Epilogue** contains lots of practical information, suggestions, and strategies that can help you make the most of all the important astrological periods that occur in your lifetime.

· ◆ · · · ◆ · ·

It's time for the mid-term (*i.e.* mid-life) report cards.

ALICE'S AND DON'S MID-TERM REPORT CARDS

There's no question that Alice and Don have both been working the curriculum over the past several years. It's taken each of them to new places in their lives, places that reflect a deepening understanding of who they are and how they want their lives to unfold. As the mid-life energies finish their passages, Alice and Don find themselves in places that bear testimony to their efforts, although a glance back over the past dozen-or-so years would reveal that the journey for each has had its twists and turns and, yes, even dead ends.

ALICE'S MID-TERM REPORT CARD

Had Alice been keeping the journals that chronicle her midlife, single life during the years she was still married to Tony, they would have revealed a life- and spirit-numbing period between her First Saturn Return, when she sat crying over her pre-dawn coffee in the luxury of her suburban homestead, and the time when, seven years later, her husband told her he had to take a break from their marriage to "find himself." The truth, of course, was that years before he had found the life he was leaving for and the person he wanted to share that life with.

It's not that Alice hadn't tried to unravel the mystery of the derailment of her "perfect" life. There had been conversations and questions; accusations and denials; long silences masked by parental activities and the pace and practicalities of managing an upward-ly-mobile domestic life. She had been lost, unconsciously doing what she figured she was supposed to do, and happily wrapped up in the maternal role she had pretty much inadvertently assumed in those times when having children was much more a natural expec-tation than a considered decision. Alice had allowed and encour-aged herself to believe what she was told; to stifle the voice of her gut's truth; to try to become only better and better at the wife/ mother role, even though she had not a single clue or standard for what defined its success. And she didn't even know what she didn't know...until that fateful day when she and Tony left the house for the tennis court to play a game of doubles and returned, each on the way to being part of a doubles team no more.

At age thirty-seven, Alice had spent the last seven-plus years in a holding pattern, trying to keep together something she knew wasn't right at age twenty-nine. She certainly didn't realize it at the time, but Tony made his big announcement only weeks away from Saturn's first important post-return checkpoint.

Mercifully, she's handled the shocking, unexpected, sudden upheavals to the status quo in unexpected fine style, especially considering what a "good girl" she has always been. She's made important moves in the direction of creating a life for herself that reflects who she is (think of her housing choice) and how she can create her own independence (that hugely significant give-back of some of her alimony.) And she's carving out time for herself, with her journals and some modest social moves. (Uranus is thrilled that astrology is involved – Uranus always likes the weird stuff.)

Neptune raises some concerns. That languid seven-year drift in the status quo looked a lot like escapism and wasted valuable time that could have moved Alice farther forward into her own life. It's hard to ignore that. But she did eventually get going, and she is doing the inner work now, too, pouring her unconscious into that journal, learning to trust her inner vision. She's definitely making a turnaround to the positive (if only she'd quit smoking!)

Saturn takes it all in, adds his contribution and delivers the mid-term over-all grade. Saturn is even less tolerant than Neptune when it comes to that seven-year productivity gap. Yes, Alice was busy being responsible: to her kids, to her husband, to her home, to her roles as the Second Grade room mother and Brownie troop leader – to everyone and everything but herself. (Neptune chimes in here with its reminder that "Workaholism can be as much escapism as a bottle of cabernet.") But – and the "but" is a big one – she sure hit the ground running once she got started.

The girls are doing well. Alice went back to school herself and got the credential she needed for a job that lines up big-time with her capabilities, and delivers great potential to become satisfying and self-supporting. She's keeping the domestic boat afloat, and gets an A+ on the housing decision.

Bottom line: Alice has moved up a whole grade-level since the First Saturn Return. She gets a B+.

DON'S MID-TERM REPORT CARD

Don sure hasn't let the grass grow much under his feet. Of course, at the time of his First Saturn Return, as a ministerial student, he believed he was only a couple of years away from planting the flag on a life-achievement summit, anticipating an especially commendable triumph considering the long odds against him.

He did everything he could during the next several years to try to stabilize life for himself and his family, though his efforts were often frustrated and thwarted by upheavals – some very dramatic – at home.

Oddly enough, leaving the seminary to teach had been the easiest part, though looking at it objectively, it had been quite a nightmare. Coping with Jean's – and the pastor's – and the congregation's – stunned disappointment and feelings of betrayal had been bad enough. But he had to immediately start making money *and* start going to school again to get his teaching credential, without totally abdicating his roles as husband and father. Miraculously, he had somehow managed to pull it off.

Almost.

The focus and energy required to execute the dramatic career and financial shifts of gear were monumental, and totally absorbing. Fulfilling his responsibilities as the family breadwinner was a daunting proposition that necessitated a return to his position as a documentation supervisor, a job that ill-suited his personal nature and barely fulfilled his financial obligations. In spite of grants and loans, the educational costs to re-tool for a new career were enormous, and only through the grace of the generosity and benevolence of his old boss had he been able to incorporate the student teaching required to complete certification.

But the price for it all was paid in the personal coin of domestic and familial distress. As young Bobby's behavioral issues intensified, and baby Laurie grew to become a soul-mate cohort for her brother, Jean's attempts at control grew increasingly chaotic and harsh. Don, absorbed in his efforts to change course, and paralyzed by the violent echoes of his own youth, provided little amelioration and comfort. At the end, there was nothing left to do but to leave with his son, and with hope, albeit faint, for a continuing presence in his daughters' lives.

The mid-life passages flow now through a once-again hardscrapple phase of life for Don, but he's patching something together and has nowhere to go but up.

Uranus applauds Don's decision not to stay in the pastoral career track once he realized that it was not for him. He had chosen it in good conscience, and integrity demanded that he own his mistake and correct course.

Neptune steps in with her message of workaholism and busyness as escapism from his responsibilities in the face of escalating domestic instability, but awards extra points for the compassionate rescue of his son. Looking for a moment into the future, we see Don entering therapy to help him sort out and make sense of his life and his choices, and to help him rise to the best he can be in his parental role for all his children. The planets all love that, but can't use it for the mid-term report card.

Saturn wishes that Don had organized and managed the practicalities of life and finance better, and worries about the brakes on that fifteen-year-old car, but commends his work ethic and commitment to make things right for himself and his family. But has Don taken on too much? Does he have a plan that can work? Has he even given thought to the idea that he needs a plan? The jury's out.

Saturn, not a planet known for generosity or free rides, lets Don keep his B...barely.

As we know, this is not a contest...and the race is far from over.

ENTR'ACTE: MY CHILD, THE POSTER CHILD – NIKKI, AGE 43

The caller ID displayed "Nikki, Work." It was all I could do to pick up the phone. For the past several months the intensity and frequency of these calls had accelerated dramatically as Nikki tried to hold on to a situation that had become unbearable. Her pain and anxiety were spilling into all corners of her world, giving her – and those who loved her – precious little peace of mind.

After college, Nikki had moved forward step-by-step, building a career and life that was by any standard a growing success. Knowing that she had no taste for the responsibilities and pressures of climbing the corporate ladder in the competitive world of Manhattan big business, she had set out to enter the elite circle of executive assistants who could make six-figure salaries attending to the needs and idiosyncratic demands of powerful CEOs and ranking executives, but leave it all at the office when she went home at the end of the day. At age thirty-seven, she landed her dream job, working for the head of a red-hot digital advertising agency which was based in Brooklyn's hip, trendy Dumbo neighborhood. She commuted only a couple of subway stops from her Park Slope co-op, except for the days when she took her boxer Argus to play with the other dogs that showed up regularly to scamper about in the free-wheeling, creative warehouse environment. She had taken a small cut in pay, but jeans had replaced Manhattan's business suits, and work didn't even begin until 10 AM. It was all perfect – a culmination of almost twenty years of hard work and moving through almost a dozen positions to better her salary, skills, and span of authority.

But a worm was burrowing into her Big Apple dream and his name was Mike. All the attention and quick money of success had gone straight to the head of her mid-thirtyish, organizationally inexperienced boss, and as his star threatened to pale in comparison to the latest up-and-coming newbies, his demands had escalated way beyond reason, and his arbitrary, ill-considered decisions were creating havoc. And it was his right-hand woman, Nikki, who was receiving the insulting, demeaning brunt of it all. Halfway into the mid-life passages, Nikki was getting a big message about a needed correction in her life course, but it was touch and go as to whether she would hear it and act on it.

The last straw came when Mike berated her in front of the general staff for not stacking water bottles properly in his office fridge, something that was not even her responsibility by an almost-twenty-years-in-the-business long-shot.

"I can't take it, Ma. Not another minute."

I could hear the tears in her voice. She was calling from a stall in the ladies' room.

"But we just bought the place upstate, and we have two mortgages. And if I leave this I'll have to suit up and go into Manhattan again. And no way will I find another place to bring Argus to work or wear jeans. And..."

Her litany of concerns was as diverse as it was long and circular. Was this going to be another false start?

Thankfully, it was not.

After waiting a couple of hours to calm down and accommodate her astrologer-Mom's timing concerns, Nikki put the current date on the long-ago composed resignation letter, walked into Mike's office and gave her notice. Here's what happened in only one year since that great day. She

- asked for and received a severance package in recognition of her five-year contribution to the company;

- was approached during her two-week notice period to rejoin a company she had twice left for a better job, to support an ex-boss who had received a big promotion;

- declined that offer and, with the urging and support of her husband Isaac, voted herself six months off to spend upstate in the country and sort things out about her future;

- got asked to bake a dozen pies for a neighbor's house-warming party and so launched a growing business right out of her farmhouse kitchen, doing something she loves;

- virtually eliminated the migraines, health scares, tears, and anxieties that had been almost constant companions;

- discovered that Isaac is indeed the great match she knew he was when she married him, and was thrilled when he was asked by his Manhattan firm to work a couple of days a week from home in order to free up some office space;

- boosted the family finances by finding someone to rent a room in the practically-vacated Park Slope apartment; and

- (icing on the cake) was asked to do part-time virtual, off-site assistant work for a small creative group that had left her former employer because of the stressful, chaotic work environment.

I don't like to think of how her life would be if she hadn't stepped up to the mid-life challenges. I thank my lucky stars that I don't have to.

The ups and downs and the work of growing and becoming continue for Nikki, as it does for all of us. It is my great blessing to be her mother and to get to witness it.

CHAPTER 5

SECOND SPRING: THE SECOND SATURN RETURN

(AGES 58-62)

"But this is what happens when we turn sixty. Random stars form constellations full of personal meaning."

RICHARD RUSSO [1]

Y OU'VE ENTERED YOUR FIFTIES AND ARE ALREADY DEALING WITH SOLICI- tations for A.A.R.P. membership. Senior citizen discounts on movie and train tickets, and Medicare and Social Security enroll- ments are just around the corner. In other words, the world has been hinting broadly that you are in what Harry Belafonte elo- quently called "the springtime of (your) winter years." The time has come to think about who you are and what you will become once you are no longer defined by what you do for a living and/or your responsibilities to anyone other than yourself.

In our society and in our times – in a culture that tries to deny the aging process through medicine and media – getting older is something that's supposed to happen to someone else. Never to us. No wonder that it can be hard to recognize that the Universe is making its own announcement, telling us that we're holding a win- ning ticket to an energetic power ball lottery: the cosmic conver- gence of the Second Saturn Return. All we have to do is cash it in.

Between the ages of fifty-eight and sixty-two, the Cycle of Adult- hood ends and the time of life begins when we can meaningfully and consciously return to *ourselves* as the primary focus of our own lives. Still-high physical energy and life experience are converging at a point of huge opportunity, the opportunity to ramp up for what can be – what holds the *promise* to be – the best years of our life. These are years when we can relax our hold on what "ought" to be and get to know and embrace the unique, irreplaceable qualities of exactly who we are. A period is dawning when the primary order of business is to grow and enrich the best old and newly-discovered parts of ourselves; to follow our curiosity; to find new passions, and pursue old, perhaps neglected, ones. It's also a time when we can explore how we might share our legacies, one-on-one, and perhaps even one-on-many, so that we leave the footprint of our passage on life's pathways.

We are all living longer, and can expect to have at least twenty more years on this planet beyond what any previous generation could even dream of having. [2,3] In fact, the fastest growing segment of our population is the sixty-five-plus age group, and by the year 2035, one-quarter of all Americans will be part of it.[4] What's more, about one-half of all those who live to be sixty-five can expect to live beyond the age of eighty-five. [5] What's important here is that not only do you get to be the architect and designer of all those years stretching out into the future, you get the chance to make a real contribution to redefining and expanding the hitherto ignored and neglected archetype of the Elder.

THE TRANSITION YEARS

The Universe, as always, is a step ahead of us mere earth-bound mortals. During the years between the ages of about fifty-eight and sixty-two, the Universal Planetary Vitamin and Supplement Dispensary is refilling and refueling your entire energetic field – body, mind, and spirit – with a formulation calibrated specifically for you at this time of life. It is everything you need to "show up for real" in your very own life and get the third great astrological cycle off to the best possible start.

Could the knees still ache each night as you climb the stairs at the end of the day? Of course. Will the brain be hard-put to come up with the name of the town you serendipitously discovered during honeymoon meanderings in Italy and swore you would never, no, never, forget (or, for that matter, the name of the movie star of the blockbuster you saw only last weekend)? Count on it. Might you have to re-set a few of the items on the bucket list you created ten years ago? Probably.

Of course the body ages, and with that comes necessary loss, but we can choose to enhance the process instead of denying its existence or letting it hold us back. Research confirms that the brain continues to grow, learning and acquiring new skills as it tweaks and rewires cellular connections throughout our lives, providing we continue to give those brains the stimulation of curiosity and new experience.[6] If we make the choice to go forward and make the best of what is yet to be, we grow the soul by creating the space where Spirit – that death-defying, eternal part of each of us that can't be taken away by anything or anyone – can grow and evolve. To quote iconic spiritual leader Ram Dass from his post-stroke wheelchair, "(It's up to each of us to) stop feeding the drama of aging." [7]

At the launch point of the third great astrological cycle of life, the rigors of learning and preparing for adulthood are long past, and the responsibilities, pressures, and privileges of that period are diminishing and being reframed. **The challenges, wonders, and excitement of life lived from the primary perspective of one's very own authentic self await us, if we dare to step into the opportunity and make it our own. And there is help for us in amazing abundance if we do.**

Let's see how Alice and Don are stepping up to the challenge.

ALICE AT 59

The early October morning holds the soft memory of summer

more than the crisp promise of autumn as Alice steps out onto the porch of the condo that overlooks the main street of the small seaside town where she and her husband spend the summer. Right after Labor Day the center of gravity of their lives had shifted only twenty short miles inland to their year-round home, but Alice is here on her own for a week. It is the week marking her Second Saturn Return, and Alice the astrologer has big plans.

"Thank Heavens Don 'gets' me so well," she muses as she straps her knees with the elastic bandages that ease their arthritic aches on her morning walks. Dropping out periodically to spend a few days on her own, living in her own thoughts and feelings and meditations, working on her writing – it's been part of the rhythm of their marriage right from the very beginning. But this time it's different.

"What a dream come true," she thinks, as she starts the ten-minute stretching routine that has helped keep her fifty-nine-year-old, not-that-slender body limber enough for her to still be able to bend over and flatten her palms on the floor with ease. "Six months after we bought this place, the town's turnaround began. It would have been totally beyond our reach." Alice could happily think this thought every day, and usually does, thanking the Universe for this blessing still beyond belief.

Sparing her knees the two flights of stairs down to street level, she takes the elevator to the lobby, walks outside, and turns toward the ocean, only three short blocks away. Typically, the two-mile circuit of her walk takes her along a seamlessly-connected boardwalk into the neighboring town, and at the end of the return loop, out to a fishing pier. There, high above the waves that crash or lap at the ever-changing tidal line, she stands at the railing for as long as her reflections keep her. For as long as it takes to absorb the peace of being where all four of earth's basic elements converge: the sun's fire, ever-present, warm on her face or not; the earth's groundedness, felt as she runs her fingers over the wood railing; the sound and smells of the ocean's waves; the brush of air, whether as a breeze cooling her forehead or a sharp wind causing a sudden shiver. On the pier, it all comes together in a sensory overload so powerful that it can stir tears.

But today is different. Today, being high up above the water and the earth, exquisite as it is, is not good enough.

Arriving at the boardwalk, Alice turns left and heads north as usual, but stops after a short while at one of the cement-framed wood benches that face the sea. Happily, there are no fishermen on the flat-topped, rocky jetty that thrusts out into the ocean. She had been prepared to wait them out for as long as it took. Crossing the wide swath of sand, feeling her sneakers fill with each step, she heads out to the jetty where she carefully steps from rock to ever-more slippery rock. Finally, she is there, right where the fire and earth and water and air – and she – can all meet.

Alice stands silently with the soft waves of low tide lapping at the rocks below her feet, gazing out to the horizon line, hands crossed in front of her. There's no sense of time either passing or not, and any separation between her and the world her bandaged knees support her on disappears. Her eyes close. They open briefly to regain her balance, then close again. Peace. Stillness, even in the call of the gulls. Heaven, right here on earth.

"Praise be. Thanks be. Ohm..."

And so Alice honors one cycle of life ending as another begins, and welcomes the start of what she trusts will be the very best time of her life.

DON AT 59

In the 5:45AM dark of a January morning, Don awakens, as always, fifteen minutes before the alarm's buzz, so that he can slide slowly and smoothly into the new day. He lingers for a moment in a dream that is rapidly smudging around the edges and lets it slip away, deciding it was more anecdotal than significant. He hits the alarm button to quiet the impending noise, and slips carefully out of bed so as not to disturb his sleeping bride. It's his first day back at school after getting in late last night from their long-anticipated Mexican honeymoon.

"Twelve years of going steady," he thinks as he starts his morning routine. "You'd think I could have spared her the 'deer in the head-lights' look when it came to saying 'I do.' But hey, it was a big – no, a huge – thing and she knows it wasn't about second thoughts, but about being literally struck by that sacred moment."

Don lingers mid-razor-stroke, blindly gazing at his reflection in the mirror, lost in the warmth of memory until he is suddenly snapped into the present by a small nick of the blade.

It's a big week, not only at school where he'll have to pick up the threads of the various Child Study Team cases that were still open at the end of the term, but also because at the end of the week he'll be taking the final exams that will lead, at last, to his therapist certification.

Don has been in pursuit of that credential almost as long as he's been with his now-wife. It hadn't been easy to keep so many balls in the air: the important work at school; the therapy curric-ulum and practicum; maintaining the connection to his now young adult kids, while coping with the outworn but still occasional after-shocks from the demise of his first marriage – never mind working hard to get this second one off to the best of all possible starts.

"It's all finally coming together," he concludes as he loads his books and file folders into the worn leather book bag that had been Alice's first important gift to him. "In the five-or-so years until I retire from the school system, I'll be able to start finding my niche in the therapy world, feathering that professional nest until I can give it my full attention."

"Okay. Enough with the noodling around, fella! Time to hit the road!"

He returns to the bedroom. Fighting off the temptation to linger in the soft sounds and rhythms of her sleep, he gently kisses his wife on the forehead, whispers a wake-up call in her ear, and heads out to the car.

And so Don, although not consciously thinking about cycles ending and beginning, honors the moment nonetheless, with culmination, and celebration, and exciting plans for the bright future that he expects will unfold.

> The Second Saturn Return occurs approximately during our fifty-ninth year. If you did the exercise in Chapter 2 you can check your *Compass* bookmark for the approximate timing of your own particular Second Saturn Return.
>
> **The Planetary Playbook** that follows the **Epilogue** has lots of suggestions for activities and practices that you can use to make the most of this important passage.

ħ

SATURN

It makes good, common sense that Saturn, the definer and guardian of astrological life cycles, is the first to arrive at the great cosmic convergence. After all, good, common sense is what Saturn is all about. By the time the Second Saturn Return period is over, we will have had the opportunity – and assignment, in fact – to realistically review the past, evaluate the present, and plan for the future, and it's a pretty good bet that if we try the ostrich approach to the passage, we can count on something coming along in the day-to-day life that yanks our head right out of the sand.

Three other planetary influences join Saturn now, but although she was present at the First Saturn Return, the Moon is not among them. Wanting our undivided attention, and knowing we were going to be extremely busy, she stopped in during our mid-fifties to see how we were doing and to facilitate any emotional course-correction that might have been necessary well in advance of *this* important time.

Saturn's intent is always to leave things more stable and secure after his passage is completed, so the first order of business is to find out exactly what's *really* going on. In his role as the Karmic Teacher, that means that he's going to start by asking some questions. At the First Saturn Return, the core question was "Are you ready to be an adult?" At mid-life, it was "How are you doing in that role?" Now, as we stand poised to enter the period of the meaningful return to *ourselves*, the central questions are

"How did you do as an adult?" and "What's next?"

Saturn starts with the cornerstone of the lifetime curriculum, the Socratic injunction to "Know thyself," by asking us to examine the patterns of the past to find the foundation for the future:

- Did you achieve the personal and professional goals and dreams that you had?

- As life unfolded, did you tweak your plans as necessary to reflect the realities of your life and your circumstances?

- Is there any unfinished business that needs attention?

Moving to the present:

- Is there anything you need to put in place (financial security, continuing education, that health and diet regime you've been meaning to start)?

- Is there anything you're ready to off-load (like the four bedroom-three-and-a-half-bath energy, effort, and money vampire, or your role as the volunteer record keeper and treasurer for the bowling league) so that you are in the best possible shape as you cross the starting line into this next era?

There's plenty of time for dealing with any errors and omissions that you identify, so take a good, hard Saturn-realistic look at what comes up. And, oh yes, jot down a few notes...we can't ignore that "brain thing" we mentioned earlier.

Saturn now steps into his Authoritarian Parent role with a couple of really big questions:

- Have you finally assumed authority and responsibility for your own life?

- Have you freed yourself from *others'* expectations and stereotypes, and from needing their approval, not only as proof of your success, but of your self-worth? After all, if you are giving others the authority to manage and approve your life, how can you hope to make that life your own?

And, like it or not, we are starting to align with Saturn's third defining archetype, the Elder. How we make the transition to this role affects all the years that lie in our future. Will we try to stay

---

SATURN STRATEGIES

Review the past. Evaluate the present. Plan for the future. Compare where you are now with where you thought you'd be.

Set short and long term goals. Make realistic, do-able plans to achieve them. Monitor progress.

Take an inventory of resources and skills relative to your goals. Fill in the gaps.

Be responsible. Pay attention to details.

Take a hard look at both tangible and energetic clutter. Clean it up.

Create something "earthy" and tangible. Plant something.

Be patient. Saturn work takes time.

within what we hope are the safe limits of the known, or, worse, dwell in the unchangeable past, living in the space of "If only..."? Or, will we attempt to deny the passage, desperately trying to hold back time, shoveling against the tide? Even children building summertime sand castles know that the ocean will reclaim them. **The goal, of course, is to be present in our own lives where they are now, enlarging and enriching them, and making them, finally, our very own.** We have come too far to be a person who is "merely...going through the motions, living more meaningfully in memory's twilight than (in) reality's noonday sun." *(8)

Saturn's focus shifts to the future: What *is* on that bucket list, anyway (the revised one, that is – the one full of stretch, but realistically do-able, goals)? Does it include anything about giving back or leaving an other-than-monetary legacy? This is a time to broaden your perspective and cultivate awareness of being part of something greater than just yourself, a time to make use of hard-earned wisdom about what you stand for, what's really important, and what meaning is inherent in the cacophony of information and experience that assaults us all on a daily basis. What are you going to do about sharing that insight and spreading that wealth?

These are absorbing, important, issues and inquiries, definitely NOT short answer or multiple choice questions. Thinking about them and acting on your conclusions takes time, and focus, and contemplation, so it's important to create space in your life for these pursuits. And it's also important to let the Universe know that you're aware of the significance and opportunity of these times, and that you're trying to make the most of them. Mindfully creating some sort of highly personal ritual or activity that sends

---

* The quote is from Richard Russo's great American novel, *Bridge of Sighs*. Its main characters are all turning sixty and are now reconnecting, having gone their separate ways after high school. The book is all about how each of them navigates this critical passage, and is filled with extraordinary insight into life at this time of life. Check it out of the library or download it onto your digital reader. You won't be disappointed.

that message of awareness, and signals that you are accepting the challenge of becoming the hero of your very own, irreplaceable life, is just the ticket to get the Universe's wind at your back. Check the **Planetary Playbook** for some ideas to get you started.

· · ◆ · · ·

After all the Saturnian hard work, and i-dotting and t-crossing, we need to lighten up a little, which is why the Universe, in its infinite wisdom, delivers up a Jupiter Return at age sixty. As we shall see, these two planets make for odd, contradictory – but somehow complementary – bedfellows. To scramble up astrologer Dana Gerhart's observation, "Saturn wields the stick, while Jupiter dangles the carrot." [9]

♃

JUPITER

· · · DESCRIPTION · · ·

Represents: Abundance. Expansion. Generosity. Growth. Faith. Prosperity. Optimism. Benevolence. Luck.

Negative Expression: Extravagance. Pretense. Self-indulgence. Excess.

Role: Your Favorite Uncle. Old King Cole.

In astrology's medieval times, Jupiter was known as the "*Greater Benefic*," the universal source of good fortune, expansiveness, benevolence, and optimism. Centuries later, the nickname still holds up. Jupiter is extroverted and gregarious and inclusive, inviting each of us to take heed of Ralph Waldo Emerson's observation that it is a "happy talent to know how to play," and to join in at the party of life and live it to the fullest. Urging us to have new adventures, no matter what our age, and to expand our horizons to develop a broader perspective on our world and our own place in it, Jupiter is in charge of making sure we include pleasure and play on our bucket list. Its overriding intent is to help us cultivate excitement and enthusiasm for life as it is now, and for how it can be in the future.

Think of your favorite uncle, the one with the big barrel chest who throws the annual Memorial Day shindig. The night before, you call and ask him if you can bring along your three old college roommates and their wives. No problem – there's always another hot dog to toss on the grill. Back in the day, when you needed a few hundred bucks for those unexpected repairs on the old jalopy, who'd you go to? Right. And you weren't surprised when a big bear hug and "Here, kid, take this extra $50, just in case…" sent you on your way. He's the one who you could always talk to and leave feeling buoyant, like there was hope in a situation you were sure was beyond repair.

But even the Greater Benefic can have a dark side. For Jupiter the coin of that realm is excess: generosity that becomes extravagance and waste; optimism going cockeyed; confidence leading to reckless risk-taking; "Don't sweat the small stuff" morphing into a shameless heresy against the God that is in the details. However, if you don't push your luck and are careful about what you ask of that favorite planetary uncle, he can bestow gifts of hope and confidence and faith in life's meaning. Jupiter can help you bounce back after a setback and take to the road again in the pursuit of your dreams, and quarterback you in your fundamental human aspiration to become something better than what you are right now.

THE JUPITER CYCLE

Jupiter takes twelve years to spin its merry way around the zodiac and return to its unchanging natal position in your birth chart. Jupiter Return times are generally hopeful and happy times when we are asked to measure and celebrate our past twelve years of growth and expansion (optimally not in the waistline dimension), and envision new possibilities for the future. Life flows, and you can take a risk and ask the Universe for even more, as long as you're willing to do your part to make it happen. Even Jupiter, the planetary architect of the positive potential of the *Law of Attraction** knows that it takes more than just dreaming and expectation to make things happen.

Jupiter returns are often marked by happy events in the biographical life: a celebration, a promotion at work, the birth of a child, a new home. Of course, you have to keep a sense of perspective and not over-extend yourself or your expectations, so that you don't fall into the push-your-luck, grandiose excesses of Jupiter's dark side. In other words, keep paying your bills and don't count on the publisher's marketing guy to show up on the stoop with the balloons and the check.

When Jupiter comes

JUPITER STRATEGIES

Go for it. Try something new. Believe you can get it done and act on that belief.

Follow your bliss, but don't get lost. Take a calculated risk, but don't go overboard.

Don't get complacent, lazy, or over-confident.

Give yourself permission to play and enjoy life.

Take a trip. Take a course. Expand your view of the world and your place in it.

Stand in the sun. Feel its vitality. Let it spark your enthusiasm.

Watch your waistline (or any area vulnerable to excess).

---

* The Law of Attraction is the principle that thoughts and expectations influence experience; that what you focus on and believe in is what you manifest, or attract, into your life.

knocking to pay a visit at age sixty, it is coordinating its cycle, for the first time in our lives, with Saturn's. With the Karmic Teacher at its side to provide the reality-check, Jupiter offers new and renewed confidence, optimism, and spontaneity for us to add to our energetic mix, urging us to expand beyond our current limitations and self-definitions. And, at this age, we are perhaps more ready than at any other time of life to recognize one of Jupiter's less ebullient but hugely significant roles: the Seeker in quest of the meaning of life. Jupiter represents wisdom, the expansive ability to connect dots of diverse information and experience and find their significance and meaning. This is what gives shape to our lives and helps us understand our place in the world. It is why Jupiter is the planet associated with philosophy, and law, and the religious tenets that give structure to spiritual belief. Jupiter models faith, not only the faith associated with a particular philosophical belief system, but faith in the benevolence and power of the Universe and, importantly, faith in ourselves. Returning at age sixty, Jupiter helps us infuse our growing spirits with that wisdom, as it urges us to take a leap of faith into our own future.

It's no surprise that our ability to recognize, accept, and integrate Jupiter's contribution to the cosmic convergence, without going off the deep end of its excesses, is an important component of the Karmic Teacher's cycle-end report card.

THE GRAND SEXTILE

Right around the time that Jupiter arrives on the scene, another important, powerful influence starts subtly building into the birth chart, and therefore into your energetic field. The **Grand Sextile**, starting quietly at around age sixty, lasts for two years, peaking at age sixty-one. Unlike the other participants in the cosmic convergence, the Grand Sextile is not about the effects of one particular planet connecting to itself. During this once-in-a-life-time two-year-long period, by astrological calculation *every* planet, advancing over the past sixty years, has come to a position where its energy is flowing smoothly back to itself in its unchanging natal position in the horoscope. In other words, it's the quintessential energetic booster shot for each and every planet in your birth chart. For example, the Sun, representing your core personality, can shine brighter with the energy of who you are; Mars, the planet that represents your physical vitality and the ability to assert yourself in pursuit of your goals, get revitalized; Mercury, how you think and learn and communicate, gets sharpened up...and so on.

Of course, the Grand Sextile can't – and isn't meant to – roll back the sands of time and turn you into Peter Pan. Besides, you wouldn't *really* want to give up all you've experienced and become over these years, would you? **What the Grand Sextile does is to give you the *opportunity* to step into the new phase of life that is dawning with renewed faculties, energies, and enthusiasms.**

Now, here's the thing about the sextile relationship between planets. Yes, it is harmonious and energetic and characterized by ease and flow. But – and the "but" is a big one – it is the energy of *possibility*. In other words, you have to recognize it and engage it and use it to make it real. Do that, and you can count on its energies to back you up for the rest of your life, as you go for that new lease on it. Ignore or deny it, and it will simply pass on through, leaving no mark. It's kind of like topping off the gas tank in a car that's in great shape but no longer new. If you don't drive it anywhere, the gas will just sit in the tank, its potential unused. By age sixty-two, The Grand Sextile has completed its passage, leaving its energetic legacy in your hands.

Pretty "grand," huh?

· · ◆ · ·

--------------------------- ♅ ---------------------------

URANUS REDUX

We first met up with Uranus at around the age of forty-two, when it – and we – were halfway through its Cycle of Individuation, that period of opportunity to recognize and develop our own unique authenticity. At that time, we were still totally enmeshed in the business of being an adult, and pressured by the responsibilities that came with that role, so Uranus' job was to remind us that there was a unique individual at the core of all that busyness. Now, three-quarters of the way through its transit around the birth chart, it makes sense that Uranus will show up again at this all-important liminal time, when we are at the brink of being able to live from the understanding and truth of who we really are. The cards are on the table: "Know thyself. Be thyself." – or risk dying day by day, even if the body holds up until you're 105.

> **URANUS STRATEGIES**
>
> Risk change: you're ready for it. Anyway, you're simply not powerful enough to stop it. Bless necessary losses and let them go. Make room for what's coming in.
>
> Do something "out of the box."
>
> Trust the gut, but use the noggin. Uranus' bright ideas come suddenly, out of the blue. Run them through Saturn's feasibility radar.
>
> Watch fireworks.
>
> Expect resistance.
>
> Pace yourself. Don't go overboard.
>
> Stay connected. Get feedback.
>
> Do a good deed in a big way.

There are enormous riches to be mined when you know who you are, where you come from, what you stand for, and how you fit into the bigger landscape of life. Saturn and Jupiter have urged us during this passage to consciously explore these issues. Now, Uranus asks us to put serious money on the bet that we can claim the energies offered by the Grand Sextile and at last put all we've learned about ourselves into living our very own, authentic lives. Like a medieval herald, Uranus lifts his flagged horn to announce that "The best is yet to be!"

Spoiler Alert: Uranus, of course, is always happy to whip up a little chaos to get your attention if there is a disconnect between who you are and the life that you're living: a personal or health crisis; a job loss – or even a global economic recession – just when you're putting the finishing touches on your retirement plans. On the other hand, whenever it's traveling hand in hand with Jupiter, as it is at this time of life, the alchemy of simple, star-sent luck is in the air, and the odds are tipping in your favor. Who wouldn't want to grab those odds, risk a leap of faith into their own authentic future, and get to feel the calm and serenity – and excitement – that comes from having claimed their own place in their very own life?

The choice, as always, is yours. If not now, when?

··◆··

ALICE'S AND DON'S SECOND SATURN RETURN REPORT CARDS

Alice and Don have certainly not let the past fifteen years go by unnoticed. They've continued the forward motion and each stands poised – conscious or not of the symbolic significance of this period – at a point where they are happy and engaged in life, and expecting it to get only better. But make no mistake: it's taken commitment and hard work, and loss and disappointment, but there are few regrets and much to be thankful for.

ALICE'S SECOND SATURN RETURN REPORT CARD

The years between the time she sat proudly and happily in her corporate cubicle, and the moment when she stands carefully but peacefully on the jetty, have flown by seemingly in the blink of an eye for Alice. The journal that was so important in navigating her through the dark, uncertain waters following her First Saturn Return was put aside for years out of the necessities demanded by the pace and responsibilities of her life, but the story of those years is locked safely in her memory and written indelibly in her spirit.

Part of Alice's plans for this meticulously-prepared Saturn Return getaway retreat is to take a trip down memory lane. The small living room of the condo is strewn with open photo albums, calendars dating back more than fifteen years, her old journals, and a box filled with a double-decade accumulation of ticket stubs, celebration invitations, various mementoes, and a pretty staggering collection of quite ordinary small rocks, carefully labeled by time and place, that mark her travels over the years. It's all so she can trigger those memories and recreate the timeline for the past thirty years. The clutter assaults her inherent need for organization and tidiness, but when she's finished, she's trusting that she will be better able to see and understand the pattern of her life's unfolding and record it in the Second Saturn Return journal that is growing quickly, page by page, during this week. The pattern was something that she could only rarely glimpse in the day-to-day whirlwind of life: raising her girls and seeing them flourish and flower as she herself climbed the corporate ladder; discovering her passion for the occult and making time (although never enough) to pursue it; re-entering the social world and – miracle of miracles – finding Don. Memories have been flooding in: birthdays and graduations, and prom nights, and promotions, and, especially, marriages. Her own had taken place only three years ago, after more than a decade of going steady, and, just last year, she watched Sasha, her oldest, walk down the aisle to Stephen and embark on her own Cycle of Adulthood by leaving the career she'd prepared so hard for, to enter medical school and risk following new dreams.

Of course, it hadn't all been the proverbial walk in the park. There had certainly been losses through death or estrangement, relationship ups and downs, misguided or simply bad decisions, and Alice being Alice, plenty of times when she could not or would not put her own needs and goals first. Then there was the exhilaration and dread surrounding her decision to take the early retirement incentive at the career she believed would last a working lifetime, in order to venture forth and claim the far less certain career that called her. And now, as she stands on the jetty, she cannot imagine that yet another one is hovering in the wings, waiting literally to be written into the script of her life.

Uranus is proud of Alice and the courage it took for the "good girl" to finally claim a life for herself that reflects who she really is, even though it disappointed others' expectations. Alice knows, for example, that it was hard for her aging parents to understand why she left the security and stability of her corporate future to strike out on her own in her mid-fifties, as an astrologer, of all things! (Uranus, of course, can't think of a better choice.)

Jupiter loves that she had the faith and confidence in herself – and in the Universe – to take the risks that allowed her to grow in all kinds of new directions. (Unfortunately, however, that expansion has included her waistline, and something needs to be done about that.) And he applauds the fact that she's had some real fun in the bargain, as witnessed by that rock collection, and quite a few of those ticket stubs.

Even Saturn is trying hard not to smile. Of course, it's in Alice's nature to be responsible and organized, and from that perspective, if anything she's over-achieved, so there's no extra credit for that. And although points definitely get awarded for the care and attention she has given to honoring this Saturn Return, well, Alice *is* an astrologer, after all. Points would have to be subtracted if she didn't. But she *is* walking her talk, and that's important. She's set stretch goals for herself but not forgotten that here on Planet Earth, we all need to be mindful of our responsibility to take care of ourselves and our own security. Alice supported her dramatic career decision with good financial planning and strict spending controls, so she gets high marks on that count. Is she sometimes too rigid for her own good (or others' for that matter)? Honesty requires a "yes." Has she been able to claim her own authority in her own life? Certainly, but there have been unquestionable lapses along the way, both professionally and personally, and some have been costly. This is definitely still what used to be called an "opportunity area" when she was completing performance reviews for her staff. And there's that lapse of Saturnian self-discipline in the diet and health department that requires attention, although the smoking is definitely history.

But, on balance, the pros heavily outweigh the cons, and even Saturn has no doubt that, given her track record, Alice will stay on course in the upcoming years.

DON'S SECOND SATURN RETURN REPORT CARD

Don travels light in this lifetime out of both inclination and necessity born of his busyness, and an ability developed over time to feel at home in short order in often changing, often minimal surroundings. So, even if he were drawn to take the time to formally retrospect his life, the triggers that could entice memory into the present are in relatively short supply. His entire life collection of pictures and mementoes is contained in only two cartons out in the garage. And although he's never kept anything resembling a formal journal, the past is captured in the entries in his indispensable day planner, whose past years lie neatly piled next to those cartons. The pages are sprinkled randomly with his impromptu musings and writings. He stacks them up out of a certainty that he will review them someday when he has time, but the time never seems to materialize.

If we were to have access to Don's day planners, we would find that they document relentless forward motion during the years since the midlife energies passed through his chart and his life. Therapy appointments untangled the legacies of his childhood and failed marriage, and helped him heal himself and become a better parent. We would see a growing interest and commitment to psychodrama, both as a student of the modality and a group participant. Advanced degree work that first furthered his teaching competence and salary level, and then facilitated a shift to a new role as school social worker, was followed almost immediately by his enrollment in the program that would qualify him as a marriage and family therapist.

On the personal side, entries for dates and more informal times with Alice steadily take up more and more ink on the pages of each week. Debtors' Anonymous meeting entries chronicle the difficult but ultimately successful resolution of a perilous money situation that was at the risk of becoming catastrophic at the time he met Alice. The "Budgeting" section of his planner now even includes line items for a gym membership and travel, and he drives an upgraded, paid-for, maintenance-current, five-year-old car with rock-solid brakes.

Yes, there's no question that Don has made use of every last ounce of the energetic, emotional, and material resources available to him as he worked on getting his life on track, and he affirmed and honored his Second Saturn Return passage intuitively but publicly with his marriage. It's not the carefully considered, ritualized recognition that it will be for Alice, but she's the one who's the astrologer, after all.

So far, so very, very good. Jupiter and Uranus both love the way Don just keeps pushing the envelope of his own life, with optimism and a willingness to step into new and unknown terrain. And he backs up his goals and dreams for himself with whatever hard work it takes to get the job done. There's no question that he is wringing every last drop out of the Grand Sextile energetic opportunity, and odds are that he's not going to stop.

Saturn, having kept his own counsel until the very end as usual, steps forward now and affirms Don's progress. His achievements in so many evolving and emerging roles required all manner of Saturnian qualities: planning, resource and time management, dedication, hard work, and responsibility.

But the matter of his children raises concerns. Although intentions were impeccable, results are at best mixed, and results do count. Young, smart Bobby never finished high school – or his naval enlistment, for that matter. Although he's on his own now, and living what appears to be an adult life, he never really acquired the emotional, educational, or psychological resources that anyone needs in order to have even a fighting chance at becoming successful in their own life. Almost as soon as Bobby moved out, Don was once again called to the rescue, this time scooping up his youngest child Laurie when mother/adolescent daughter antagonisms reached unbearable levels. Once again he found himself in the role of single parent, this time of an angry, emotionally volatile teenage girl, and once again, he did everything he could think of to help her. With experience and his own growth as a back-up, Don quarterbacked Laurie as she strove for and achieved personal and professional independence and success, something that required monumental effort on both their parts. For a long time his relationship with middle child Christine suffered, not only because she was living at the opposite end of the country, but also as a consequence of family dynamics combined with the complications and demands of Don's life. For too long, their relationship had narrowed to not much more than polite holiday and birthday exchanges and carefully orchestrated visits, but days now were marked with real progress and the gap was closing rapidly. Still, Saturn is reluctant to deduct points on the parenting issue. Saturn is, after all, the authority on the role of the authoritarian parent, and there is no question that Don gave it his all. Intent and effort matter.

Finally, as the third astrological era dawns in Don's life, there is absolutely no question that he will keep the pace he has set for himself.

Alice and Don both pull a solid A, but on second thought, Saturn makes it an A-minus. He always likes to leave room for improvement.

Stay tuned...the best is yet to be.

--- ∞ ---

ALICE AND DON: A VERY GOOD LIFE

"And I think of my life as vintage wine
from fine old kegs.
From the brim to the dregs
It pours sweet and clear.
It was a very good year."

"IT WAS A VERY GOOD YEAR"
ERVIN DRAKE, COMPOSER

The tour bus pulls into the parking lot at the eastern corner of the rainforest that covers more than a quarter of the mid-winter sun-struck Caribbean island. The doors open and, one-by-one, for the third time this day, the passengers descend, most of them gingerly, encouraged and aided by the smiling, island-proud tour guide. It's a pretty homogeneous group, broken up only by a sprinkling of middle-aged vacationers, a pair of honeymooners (who are prob-ably going to have quite a chat with their travel agent once they get home), and a couple with what looks like an sixteen-or-so year-old son who is sulking every step of the way, angrily pounding at his portable electronic game station.

"Now, remember," says the guide, once the group has reassem-bled at the entrance to the park, "it's a long, steep way down to the pool. Don't try to go down there unless you're absolutely certain you can make it back. There are plenty of observation platforms along the way where you can stop, but the elevators are out of order."

The laughs come right on cue. The group is all about joviality in the face of the unrelenting march of time – for today, anyway.

"Now, get out those umbrellas, folks," continues the cheerleader, "that big gray cloud is about to break loose!"

Alice smiles as she digs out the sunflower-yellow umbrella from the bottom of her canvas tote bag. "If someone told me twenty years ago that I'd be happy to be on a tour bus with a bunch of what my Dad used to call 'Old Duffers' and their wives," she thinks, "I'd not only have thought they were nuts, I'd have been ticked off and insulted. But I love this mid-winter, bone-warming annual getaway, and so does Don. We're both so busy and work so hard. We need this time together. And if it puts us on this tour bus with some 'Old Duffers,' well, so be it: they remind me of Dad."

She had pushed for the tour after she read in the excursion brochure that the stream running through the pool at the bottom of the tropical extravagance of the rainforest was reputed to be the source of the Fountain of Youth. Don, although unrelentingly averse to anything resembling structured recreation in herding groups, had agreed to go out of love – and a reluctance to *not* cover all his bets.

Snapping open the umbrella, Alice sets off on the path, following the leisurely pace set by the guide, with Don right behind her, standard male umbrella-bearing aversion behavior in full flower, getting inundated.

"He always has my back," Alice thinks, and reaches back to squeeze his hand.

About a third of the way down, with less than half the group still in tow, the guide musters a check-in at an observation deck.

"It gets really steep from here on," she announces, "and this is pretty much your last chance at a comfortable stopping point. Do any of you want to continue?"

Alice, strapped knees aching from the slippery descent, and still needing to climb back to the waiting bus, steps out to the railing to get a good observation point. At least half of the remaining group turns back for the sharp ascent to the gift shop at the edge of the parking lot. Only two people step forward: Don and the teenager.

"Don...is he nuts?"

"Are you sure you can make it? It's awfully steep."

"I'll know if I have to turn back."

"Well, watch out for those tree roots...they're slippery!"

"Sure..."

And down he goes, preceded by the sixteen-year-old and followed by the guide. The small party disappears in the foliage for a long while, reappearing at the bottom of the canyon more than five long minutes later.

Don looks up and, thanks to her jaunty umbrella, spots Alice right away, high up in the mist. He signals a thumbs up.

Imagining his proud grin, she swings the umbrella back and forth over her head in response.

The boy has long before dived into the pool and is swimming toward the waterfall that defines its far end. Don makes his way carefully through the rocks and roots that line the pool's borders. He steps in up to his knees and dips his hands in, then reaches up to splash water over his head, repeating the pattern a half dozen times or more. Don turns to the shore, and then hesitates and goes back, grabbing his water bottle out of the back pocket of his shorts. He empties the bottle on land, turns, and lets water from the pool bubble in to refill it. He screws the top back on and turns to the call of the guide, who is ready to start the ascent.

The teenager reluctantly joins the party and they are soon once again lost in the moist green mists of the rainforest.

Finally, Don arrives at the deck where Alice is waiting, towel in hand.

"Wait a minute," he smiles. "Take off that straw hat."

She gives him a quizzical look, and then gets it.

He unscrews the cap of the water bottle and pours its contents over her head.

And so Alice and Don celebrate the moment they are living in, welcoming each day of what they *know* to be the best time of their lives.

EPILOGUE

Through the Looking Glass
Afterword – A True Story
Prologue: The Circle of Life – Lulu at 12

THROUGH THE LOOKING GLASS

I N STATELY SLOW CADENCE OR BRIGHT UP-BEAT TEMPO – OR AT SOME-
thing in between – the planets continue their eternal circuits
into an endless future. For as long as we live, each will continue to
make important contacts to our birth charts, providing a bottom-
less source of energetic potential that we can use to stay alive and
growing until our very last breath.

At about age sixty-six or sixty-seven, Saturn connects back to
itself so we can check in on how well we've launched his third cycle.
At seventy-two, the planetary odd couple arrive together again,
Saturn half-way through its circuit; Jupiter kicking off another
twelve-year cycle of growth and expansion. In our mid-eighties,
several muster up once again in a really big way:

- Neptune hits the half-way point of its 167-year cycle,
- Jupiter launches its eighth twelve-year cycle at age eighty-four,

- Uranus finishes its eighty-four-year circuit of the birth chart, thereby completing the Cycle of Individuation, and
- Saturn arrives for its third return at about age eighty-seven.

And so it goes...each of the planetary allies we've met in this book – and their cohorts – check in, bringing renewed possibilities for growth and wisdom, joyful, hopeful and exciting times, and times of change and quiet – until, finally, we move out to the astral plane to regroup and plan for the next lifetime.

For now, just keep up the good work. These are the best of times.

AFTERWORD – A TRUE STORY

Youth is a gift of nature.
Age is a work of art.

- STANISLAW LEE
(AND MY DAD'S FAVORITE QUOTE)

My Dad was eighty-four and a half when my Mom died after a long and grueling illness that absorbed both their lives during the last three or four years of hers. Still, during that time, he insisted that my sister and I "Stand back!" and step forward with help and support only upon request.

Within a month of her passing, he was behind the wheel of a new car, one clean of painful reminders of the eight-cylinder behemoth that had accommodated her necessary medical equipment. Before long, sounding an echo of times spent as a reporter on his college newspaper, he was writing a personal essay column for his community's monthly newsletter, a column that quickly gained huge popularity among his like-aged neighbors. Cameras were going digital and, as a lifelong photography buff, he invested in a state-of-the-art model and lessons for its use. Within a few months, he was, with my sister's and my heartfelt encouragement (he had charmingly and diffidently checked in with us first), dating Margaret, a cultured, beautiful "Shadow Laker" like himself who was a dead-ringer for Mom.

Dad died five years after my mother, on an April day that had started with a scramble-up of his favorite kielbasa and egg breakfast, a week or so after getting cataract surgery so that when the golf season started he could refine his game.

If he wasn't my own Dad, I wouldn't believe it.

This is all I have to say about how the Cycle of Individuation is never really complete.

PROLOGUE: THE CIRCLE OF LIFE
LULU AT 12

I love that my granddaughter was born in the year 2000. For one thing, it helps me keep track of her age. But more importantly, she – and her cohorts – represent the hope of the future in this new millennium.

I love that her full name is "Lucera," Italian for the "Little Light," because that is what the world needs more of in these intense times – clarity and light.

Boys and girls born since the mid-'90s are sometimes called *crystal children*, and as I watch Lulu grow up, I see many of the qualities associated with that generation emerging in her personality. She's sensitive, affectionate and loving; musically-oriented (she plays the piano, the clarinet, and the cello, and can carry a tune, which no one else on the Loffredo side of her family can do); artistically gifted (she is never without a sketch pad, and her drawings and paintings attract attention, and even awards); forgiving of others; helpful and caring, especially to those who need it; attuned to animals and nature (Be careful not to inadvertently step on an ant colony when she's around!); has a great sense of balance and a fearless love of climbing (rock-climbing is one of her favorite summer camp activities); and, even at this young age, Lulu is a vegetarian.[*] But all this does not mean that Lulu is not 100% "'tween," these days, entranced with make-up and hair styles and fashion, knowing Selena Gomez's favorite ice cream flavor, every last detail about Taylor Swift's love life, along with the lyrics to all their songs. She giggles and whispers with her girlfriends, and is interested, uncertain and shy about boys, but has completely disarming moments

---

[*] The crystal characteristics are drawn from Doreen Virtue's book *The Crystal Children*. See the Bibliography for publishing details.

when she's still that little girl who loved to hang out and color with her Meema (that's me), and didn't want to know how the Christmas surprises showed up under the tree.

Of course, the experiences and decisions that are the subject of this book are far in the future for Lulu right now. Her job is to live in the moment and explore all that she is. But hopefully, when the time comes, as it will, she can pick up this book and find some guidance and help, and the voice of her Meema, in it.

THE PLANETARY PLAYBOOK

A COLLECTION OF IDEAS FOR MAKING THE MOST OF THE TIMES OF YOUR LIFE

Life Timeline
Get Read
Make Time for Good Time
Put These Quotes on your Refrigerator Door
Take a Trip Down Memory Lane
Ask Good Questions... Find Good Answers
Create a Ritual
Write an Ethical Will (Second Saturn Return)
Look for Help to Show Up

HAD THE PLANETS THAT GUIDE AND SUPPORT US THROUGH THE GREAT evolutionary passages of our lifetimes held a brainstorming session to come up with ideas and suggestions to help make the most of them, they might have come up with **The Planetary Playbook**. It starts with a timeline that identifies the ages when consideration of these ideas can be particularly helpful.

· · ◆ LIFE TIMELINE ◆ · ·

AGE (APPROXIMATE)	LIFE EVENT (COMPASS REFERENCES)	PLANETARY EVENT (SEE "ASK GOOD QUESTIONS. FIND GOOD ANSWERS." SECTION OF THIS PLAYBOOK)
27-29	Cycle of Preparation Ends, Adulthood Begins (Chapter 3)	Progressed Lunar Return First Saturn Return
40-44	Midlife Passage (Chapter 4)	Uranus Opposite Uranus Neptune Square Neptune Saturn Opposite Saturn
58-62	The Cycle of the Meaningful Return to the Self Begins (Chapter 5)	Second Saturn Return Jupiter Return Grand Sextile Uranus Square Uranus
Looking Ahead		
Age 72	Mid-Cycle	Saturn Opposite Saturn Jupiter Return
Ages 84-88	The Cycle of Individuation Culminates (Epilogue)	Neptune Opposite Neptune Jupiter Return Uranus Return Third Saturn Return

GET READ

First, a pitch for the home team. The energetic passages marking evolutionary milestones move through every person's chart at the same chronological age, but the charts – and people – they move through are totally unique. This means that the energies play out differently for each individual, stimulating personal planets and configurations, and emphasizing different areas of life experience. For example, at the Second Saturn Return, if natal Saturn is in the part of the birth chart representing partnership and marriage (*i.e.* The Seventh House*), much of the learning and growth that occurs will be in the arena of committed partnerships. One thing's for sure: you will be asked to take a very realistic look at the relationship and make any necessary adjustments, because Saturn simply has no tolerance for rose-colored glasses. Place the natal Saturn in the part of the chart having to do with career and life direction (*i.e.* The Tenth House*), and … well, you can finish this sentence.

The fact is that there's no better time than *any* present moment to get a professional reading of your astrological birth chart. Not only will you deepen your understanding of yourself and your own unique energetic palette of possibility, but if significant generational passages are occurring, they can be woven into the total picture.

Word of mouth referral is definitely the best way to go when it comes to finding the right person. You'll need the DATE, TIME, and PLACE of your birth when you make the appointment. And yes, the TIME is a critical piece of information.

MAKE TIME FOR GOOD TIME

At the times of major generational passages, so much is going on that it can feel like you're at the Fourth of July fireworks on The Mall in Washington, DC. Some planets shine brighter, sound louder, and blare longer than others, but it all adds up to a spectacular conflagration of exciting, confusing, contradictory energetic

---

*   For an explanation of the houses and what they represent, see "More About the Birth Chart" in the Appendix.

explosions. However, The Mall at our nation's capitol on Independence Day is exactly NOT the environment that's needed to successfully navigate these important times.

Rather, we need to immerse ourselves in **kairos**, which is the Greek word for time that is not measured by the clock. Anchored in the peace and clarity of the eternal present of *kairos*, we can move through its open doorway to the place where Universal wisdom and consciousness reside. These are the energies that can help us make sense of the past and guide us to our own best future. Buddhist monk Ajahn Sona, quoted by Joan Borysenko and Gordon Dveirin in *Your Soul's Compass,* [1] says it eloquently and succinctly: "Most problems are not to be solved, but dissolved by silence and clarity." I would only add that deep realizations, opportunities, and other insights are also recognized in that same space.

In our day and age, speed rules and seems to accelerate exponentially beyond our capacity to integrate the pace. The modern world's values don't grant high status to reflection and contemplation, so we need to retreat from that world to a place where we can get to the present moment and find *kairos*. How you define and spend your discretionary time is obviously in your own hands, which means that you have to *choose* to find *kairos*. Figure out what works best for you. Not everyone needs absolute silence in a darkened, interior space. Some may need music, others to be out in nature. There are those who can informally create space in their day for *kairos*, but for many, conscious scheduling is an imperative. If you're one of those many, set aside way more time than you thought you'd ever need and then add 25% more. And, either way, consider this: The boundaries that separate us from the peace and wisdom of the Eternal are thinnest in the early morning and at night.

But please, whatever you do, before you add another "app" to your interactive phone, consider whether it's going to make time for *kairos* or take it away.

PUT THESE QUOTES ON YOUR REFRIGERATOR DOOR

☆

"A strong intent is the single most important requirement to bring about growth and change."

(Just don't forget to back it up with
good, solid work and effort.)

☆

"It's not the events that matter. It's what you do with what happens to you that counts."

(This is a paraphrase from Dane Rudyer, whose thinking revolutionized and modernized astrology in the 20th century, but I think I've seen it attributed to others as well. Wherever it comes from, it's important.)

☆

"Negative thinking doesn't get you anywhere but stuck."

(In other words, positive expectations and optimism are the strongest consistent predictors of positive results…. as long as you do the necessary work, that is.)

TAKE A TRIP DOWN MEMORY LANE

The landscape of your unique past holds patterns that can help you understand the present and create a vision for the future. Relatively few of us keep organized – or even randomly-annotated – histories of that past. Whether or not you are one of those few, an amble down the personal passageways of memory holds the promise of great satisfaction and rewards, not only from what is discovered, but from the simple act of doing it.

Use the information and recollections you come up with to create a timeline for your past, and use the insights from all your resources to see if you can detect any patterns. Take notes.

- What were you *feeling* about the memories that came up?

- Were there dreams that got lost in the shuffle?

> ### MEMORY TRIGGERS
>
> Gather up journals and photo albums and review them.
>
> Check your *Compass* bookmark dates. What was happening?
>
> Think of favorite books and movies and use the internet to see when they came out.
>
> What big news events do you remember? What were you doing when they happened?
>
> Draw a map of your childhood neighborhood or the one where you had your first grown-up apartment.
>
> Think back to memorable family events. When did cousin Mary get married to that guy nobody liked? When did you take your kids on their first trip to Disney?
>
> Think of holiday celebrations.

- Did certain mistakes get repeated again and again?

- What have you always wanted more – or less – of?

- What have you always really cared about?

- What would you nurture and hope to grow more of in yourself? What would you change?

Now, check your personal timeline against the planetary one at the start of the **Playbook**. How does it line up? Use the information in *Compass* to identify lessons that might be learned from the planetary passages that occurred at important times in your biographical life. This helps you take optimum advantage of passages that are still on the horizon. For example, if there was the launch of a new Jupiter cycle, what can you remember about any new period of growth and expansion that started around that time? How can you gear up to maximize the opportunities for forward motion when Jupiter revisits your chart?

The trip down memory lane can warm your heart, fire up your enthusiasms, and bring important insights into how you can marshal your talents and abilities to get yourself where you want to go.

ASK GOOD QUESTIONS... FIND GOOD ANSWERS

Each member of the planetary team has ideas to share from its own particular perspective – questions and strategies to consider when it stops in for a visit. This list is simply to get the ball rolling... you'll come up with your own additions and variations.

At the end of the process, go quiet, find *kairos*, and listen for the voice of your heart and spirit. There you go...all questions answered.

JUPITER	
QUESTIONS	STRATEGIES
How can I expand and grow in a positive direction? Have I stretched myself fully to my highest potential?	Go for it. Try something new. Believe you can get it done and act on that belief. Trust yourself...and the Universe. It's got your back.

JUPITER

QUESTIONS	STRATEGIES
What gives me true pleasure and makes me feel alive? How can I bring more of this into my life?	Follow your bliss, but don't lose track of the details.
Have I hoped for – asked for – enough out of life? Am I cheating myself?	Take a calculated risk, but don't go overboard.
Do I have faith in myself? If not, what can I do to build it?	Don't get complacent, lazy, or over-confident.
Am I proud of myself and my accomplishments without getting too "full" of myself?	Give yourself permission to play and enjoy life.
Am I being generous – or is it reckless extravagance? Am I being irresponsible? Has my optimism gone cockeyed?	Take a trip. Take a course. Expand your view of the world and your place in it.
	Stand in the sun. Feel its vitality. It will spark your enthusiasm and optimism.
	Watch your waistline (or any area vulnerable to excess).

THE MOON

QUESTIONS	STRATEGIES
Am I in touch with my emotional nature and reactions? Do I allow myself to feel what I really feel? How do I *feel* about myself and my life?	Spend quiet time alone in familiar, comfortable surroundings. Listen for the voice of your feelings.
What are my emotional wounds? How can I heal them?	Watch a movie or read a book that touches your heart. Browse through your children's baby pictures, or your own. Hug your pet, if you have one. How do you feel?
Do I trust my intuition and instincts?	

THE MOON

QUESTIONS	STRATEGIES
Do unconscious behaviors and instincts "run the show" without my being aware of them?	Stand out in the moonlight and just soak it up.
Am I able to give myself what I need? Can I then nurture and care for others? How?	Blood to the heart first: Take good care of yourself in all kinds of ways. You can't give from an empty well.
Can I share my emotions with trustworthy, caring people?	Keep a journal. Record your emotional, intuitive reactions to life's experiences.
Do I understand that others may feel differently than I do? Do I respect their feelings?	Learn to trust your gut. Start with baby steps and build confidence.
Am I in touch with my family and roots as sources of love, support, and identity, without being blocked or confined by them?	Seek therapy to help understand yourself and to heal wounds. Try to re-connect with family members if uncomfortable distance has developed.

NEPTUNE

QUESTIONS	STRATEGIES
What dreams do I have for myself and those I love?	Unite body, mind and spirit. Slow down. Spend quiet time in soothing, calm surroundings, or out in nature, near water. Meditate or start a yoga practice. Pray.
Do I trust my intuition?	
What don't I know about myself?	
Do I have an open, clear connection to Spirit? If not, what can I do to build one?	Envision your future. Let yourself dream a big dream.

NEPTUNE

QUESTIONS	STRATEGIES
Has "mañana" become my personal anthem? Am I drifting?	Keep a dream journal. Look for repeated patterns and symbols. What are they trying to tell you?
Can I surrender to what must be?	
Am I stuck in self-pity and "why me" consciousness? Am I really as power-less as I feel?	Do something creative. (Photography is associated with Neptune, but it's certainly not the only option.) Don't worry about what you produce: it's the doing that counts, because it brings something from within you out into the world.
Am I being truthful to myself and others?	
Do I follow my own course, or do I drift along in someone else's current?	Grieve losses and pain – they are part of the growth process. Then move on, focusing on the new opportunities on the horizon.
	Seek therapy to discover what you don't know about yourself: hidden treasures and gifts; hidden, self-de-feating saboteurs.
	Be patient with the "Neptune Fog." Clarity *will* emerge, and until it does, don't get lost in the drift.
	Very Important: Don't make big decisions until the passage is over. Wait for the clarity.
	Let yourself feel tired. Get enough rest. Neptune passages can be draining.

NEPTUNE

QUESTIONS	STRATEGIES
	Do something charitable and compassionate. Helping others stimulates Neptune's positive energy.

SATURN

QUESTIONS	STRATEGIES
Am I a responsible, adult person? Have I assumed authority for living my own life and freed myself from other's expectations and stereotypes?	Review the past. Evaluate the present. Plan for the future. At Saturn Returns or checkpoints, compare where you are now with where you thought you'd be approximately seven years ago… fifteen years ago…twenty-nine years ago. What are your conclusions?
Have I achieved earlier goals that I set for myself? What are my long-term goals? Is there a realistic, do-able plan to achieve them? What's the timeline? What are the interim goals and checkpoints to keep me on track?	Set conscious short and long term goals, and make a realistic, do-able plan to achieve them.
What unfinished business do I have to take care of? Are there responsibilities to myself and others that I have neglected?	Check in periodically to monitor progress.
Do I need to acquire additional resources? New knowledge or skills?	Take a personal inventory of resources and skills relative to your goals and responsibilities. Fill in the gaps.
Have I taken care of my long-term security needs? If not, what will I do about it?	Be responsible. Pay attention to the details.
What accomplishments am I proud of?	

SATURN

QUESTIONS	STRATEGIES
What lessons have I learned? What's on my bucket list? Is it do-able? How? Are there any additions? Deletions?	Take a hard, realistic look at both tangible and energetic clutter, and create a plan to clean out the metaphorical personal garage. Get mentoring, then be a mentor. Teach and be taught. Leave a legacy. Give back. Pass the torch. Make something "earthy" and tangible and real, something you can point to and take pride in. Plant a flower in the garden. Be patient. Saturn work takes time.

URANUS

QUESTIONS	STRATEGIES
How does the life I'm living personally and professionally stack up against the real me? Where do I feel hemmed in? Are the limitations legitimate (ex: family responsibilities)? What am I going to do about ones that aren't? If something is at risk – relationship, job, "stuff," whatever – is it more important than having a "me?" Is it really an either/or situation?	Risk necessary change: you're ready for it. Anyway, you're simply not powerful enough to stop it, and if you insist on trying, the energy spent will be wasted. Bless necessary losses and let them go. Make room for what's coming in. Open yourself up to new ideas and ways of thinking. Do something "out of the box," just to see how it feels. March to your own drummer, but remember to stay with the parade.

URANUS

QUESTIONS	STRATEGIES
Is it time to take a risk? Am I really open to change that takes me in a positive direction? If not, why? If not now, when?	Trust the gut, but use the noggin. Uranus' bright ideas and hunches come straight out of the blue, where originality and genius reside. Just be sure to run them through Saturn's feasibility radar.
Have I gone overboard? Am I alienating myself from people I care about in the name of my own freedom? Have I butted into *their* lives too much with my own agendas?	Watch fireworks.
	Expect resistance. Others may be threatened by the trails you're blazing and, after first digging in their heels, might turn on them and go. Remember, space is being made.
What would Einstein – or my best friend – have to say about this situation?	Stay connected. Don't let Uranus' cool, detached objectivity go to extremes and disconnect you not only from others, but from your own heart.
	Do a good deed in a big way. Humanitarian activities can calm Uranian edginess, and you'll do some good in the bargain.

CREATE A RITUAL

Personal, private rituals send messages of consciousness and dedication to the Universe. They are practices full of mystery and power. Coming out of a deep, special place within us, their power lies in how they connect us to a mysterious "something" that is much greater than ourselves, something so vast that it's even hard to find the right words to describe it. With repetition, that link strengthens. Because rituals demonstrate that we're awake and present in our lives, the Universe loves them and responds with guidance, support, and protection.

Rituals are particularly powerful when we are at threshold moments in our lives, times when we are no longer totally in our old state of being, but not yet totally in the new. They open the door to the Eternal and Its wisdom, guidance, and support. You can see why creating a ritual at the particular time of an important generational passage can be so important. Here are some ideas to get you started. The details are – have to be – up to you.

- **Keep it private.** Solitary, self-contained presence is fundamental to personal ritual. You are taking the ordinary and sanctifying it, which literally means transforming it into the sacred. Your undisturbed presence in the moment is absolutely required. That having been said, it doesn't mean you can't invite someone to contribute, someone whose presence adds meaning and depth to the experience. Just make sure *you* plan the level and timing of the participation.

- **Make it personal.** Rituals don't have to be big and elaborate or cost a lot. The only core requirement is that they be a reflection of you, not some "one size fits all" generic yawn appropriated from pop culture or New Age folderol. Incorporate meaningful-to-you objects and practices. Gather up protective talismans and charms, and mementos that tie to you important people, places, traditions, and experiences in your life. If it feels right, use them to create an altar or shrine, or carry them close.

Artistic or decorative talent is not at all important, but aesthetics are. The environment should be pleasing to *you* – the location; the placement of objects; the pattern and texture of fabric; the color, scent, and shape of a candle. And if you include music, be sure it's music that makes *your* heart sing. Enya and Gregorian chant are great, but so is Tchaikovsky – or even Neil Diamond. Silent reflection and uninterrupted presence and awareness are fundamental, but so is singing and chanting...or dancing...or whirling, if you're a dervish. And add anything that arises spontaneously in the moment: the impulse is coming from a sacred place.

- **Give thanks.** Reflect on what you're grateful for. Start with "for being alive..." and go on from there. Write it all down... or sing it out...or shout it out. Whatever the medium, deliver your message of awareness and thanks for blessings great and small. Gratitude for what you've received allows the Universe to send even more.

- **Invite the Universal.** Here on Planet Earth, it's not always easy to remember that we are spiritual beings that have incarnated in the elemental fire, earth, air, and water of human life. One way to put it all back together – to link our humanity to that wondrous, unnamable and indescribable mystery – is to incorporate something in your ritual that acknowledges this truth. Find a place out in nature where you can optimally stand in the presence of its elements, where your human senses can experience them simultaneously. Or, incorporate them symbolically in your ritual practice: drink a sip from a glass of pure spring water and pour the rest into the houseplant on your kitchen window sill as you stand in the sunbeam that brightens the breeze coming in through that open window. Just take it all in. Go where it all takes you. You won't get lost...

But you don't need any more of my ideas. You have more than enough of your own.

WRITE AN ETHICAL WILL (SECOND SATURN RETURN)

Who are you? What do you believe in? What matters to you? The answers to questions like these are a more important legacy than anything you will stipulate in your legally-crafted Last Will and Testament.

Think of nature's cycle: after flowering, a plant sets its seed to store its energy for times to come. The Second Saturn Return period in the human life cycle coincides with that seed-setting, making it an excellent time to start thinking about writing the Ethical Will that will carry the light of your presence on this earth into the future.

Every single planet that has guided you to this point applauds and encourages the idea:

- **Jupiter**, the philosopher who connects dots of information into patterns of meaning, wants you to recognize those patterns in your own life, and see how that life fits into the bigger Universal picture;

- **The Moon**, who holds our feelings and ability to care for and nurture ourselves and others, knows that this process will enrich and warm your heart and soul, and the hearts and souls of those who receive this legacy;

- **Neptune**, who connects us to our own unconscious and points the way to direct contact with the Divine, also speaks to our creativity, and wants you to experience and bring forth what lies within you and share it;

- **Saturn**, the authoritarian parent and teacher, sees this as an important, responsible assignment that teaches you about yourself and enriches the wisdom of future generations; and

- **Uranus**, the guardian and defender of our individuality and freedom, wants you to know and stand strong for who you are and what you value.

The planetary team sees the writing of an Ethical Will as an opportunity not only to pass the torch, but to spend important time with yourself, and to learn even more about the totally unique, irreplaceable person you and only you are. It's not a project done in a day, but if you take that trip down memory lane as part of your Second Saturn Return practices, at the end of it you'll have a huge head start on *this* initiative.

You can buy a fancy leather-bound book, or even hire a professional ghost writer, but the format and style are not what's important. It's all about the intent, the content, and its authenticity as a statement of who *you* are, not who you are as defined by anyone else.

As always, asking yourself the right questions heads you in the best direction for the right answers, so here are a few to get you started:

- Who are you? What qualities define you? What are you proudest of?

- What do you believe in and stand for?

- Why does what's important to you matter?

- What are the most important experiences and insights you'll take with you from this lifetime?

- What do you wish you could have changed about yourself?

- Who are the important people in your life? What have you shared with them? What have you learned from them?

- What have you learned from the "school of hard knocks?"

- What regrets would you have if this were the last week of your life?

- What are your hopes and wishes for your loved ones?

- What are your most precious memories – the ones that touched your heart?

- What are your favorite quotes? Books? Music? What makes them your favorites?

- What's on your bucket list?

Finally, just a few suggestions:

- Don't give advice you're not willing to or were unable to take yourself. We're not talking theory here.

- Be sure to celebrate the life you have lived and are living – it's the most precious gift anyone ever gets and shares. And remember that the smallest, most anonymous graces matter as much as gestures painted in the broadest brush strokes.

- Share your Ethical Will when/how/with whom *you* want. Sharing it while you're still on the planet can deepen the connections to those you care most about, but the choice is definitely yours.

- Keep at it. Revisit it every now and again, according to your own timeline, perhaps when important generational pas-sages are occurring, or on an annual basis, or when events stir in your life. Make it a living document as long as you're living. Remember, the opportunity to learn and love and grow in your life *never* ends.

LOOK FOR HELP TO SHOW UP

When you are moving in the direction of your highest good, you're likely to notice that you are somehow mysteriously accessing energies greater than your own. Things seem to line up in ways that facilitate and support your growth; long shots come through; messages are delivered; *synchronicity* abounds. Synchronicity occurs when logically unrelated situations and people connect up, without apparent cause-and-effect relationship, to deliver meaningful-to-you insight and guidance.

Keep your eyes open. The signs will be there. Follow where they point. The message is clear: recognizing your commitment to your own potential, the Universe's mainsail has shifted the wind to your back.

Blessings on your way...

APPENDIX

More About the Birth Chart
Glossary
Bibliography
Chapter Notes

---------------- ----------------

MORE ABOUT THE BIRTH CHART

THE LANGUAGE OF ASTROLOGY IS BUILT FROM THREE INTERRELATED groups of symbols: planets, signs, and houses. The planets represent basic types of energy found in everyone (emotions, personality, communication style, etc.) They were introduced in Chapter 1. This section contains information about the signs and houses, and includes a discussion of how the chart is constructed.

The Signs. The twelve signs function like stained glass panels, filtering and modifying the energy released by each planet. For example, the Moon in the energetic, confident sign of Leo, is outgoing and extroverted, and expresses its feelings openly

> **Reminder:** Since all astrological symbols are neutral, but can be expressed in either positive or negative ways depending on our free will and choice, I'll alert you to some of the downside for each sign and house.

and easily. Filter the basic lunar emotions through the sign of Scorpio, and the person with that Scorpio Moon feels things deeply and intensely, and closely guards their privacy.

· · ◆ THE SIGNS ◆ · ·

NAME	DESCRIPTION	NEGATIVE EXPRESSION
ARIES	Assertive. Optimistic. Confident. Energetic. Forthright. Entrepreneurial.	Egotistical. Aggressive. "In your face." Insensitive. Impatient.
TAURUS	Grounded. Solid. Strong. Aesthetically sensitive. Practical. Natural. Patient. Thorough.	Stubborn. Materialistic. Lazy. Unimaginative. Self-indulgent.
GEMINI	Curious. Smart. Clever. Sociable. Youthful. Communicative. Flexible.	Restless. Unfocused. Inattentive. Too talkative. Superficial. Fickle.
CANCER	Sensitive. Nurturing. Caring. Kind. Emotional. Imaginative. Intuitive.	Guarded. Moody. Grudge-holding. Clinging. Suffocating. Worrying.
LEO	Generous. Playful. Optimistic. Dramatic. Creative. Romantic. Self-assured. Warm. A leader.	Vain. Extravagant. Overbearing. Attention-mongering. Self-indulgent. Pretentious.
VIRGO	Intelligent. Analytical. Detail-oriented. Studious. Hard-working. Methodical. Helpful.	Picky. Petty. Critical. Pedantic. Workaholic.
LIBRA	Sociable. Diplomatic. Peace-loving. Romantic. Cooperative. Artistic.	Wishy-Washy. Indecisive. Apathetic. Peace at any price. Self-indulgent.

· · ✦ THE SIGNS ✦ · ·

NAME	DESCRIPTION	NEGATIVE EXPRESSION
SCORPIO	Powerful. Intense. Probing. Transformative. Determined. Passionate. Courageous. Introspective.	Manipulative. Secretive. Jealous. Possessive. Vengeful. On a power trip. Intolerant. Betraying.
SAGITTARIUS	Adventurous. Freedom-loving Optimistic. Non-judgmental. Philosophical. Straight-forward.	Impatient. Unreliable. Insensitive. "Foot in mouth." Reckless. Inattentive to detail.
CAPRICORN	Ambitious. Hard-working. Responsible. Determined. Conventional. Serious. Needs to "do the right thing."	Autocratic. Domineering. Stern. Cold. Armored. Controlling. Unforgiving. Status-seeking. Workaholic. Inhibited.
AQUARIUS.	Smart. Brilliant. Intellectual. Original. Freedom-loving. Independent. Tolerant. Humane. Progressive.	Opinionated. Eccentric. Stubborn. Impersonal. Detached. Rebellious.
PISCES	Spiritual. Meditative. Introspective. Sensitive. Compassionate. Intuitive. Visionary. Creative.	Overly-sensitive. Lacking self-confidence. Apathetic. Spineless. Pessimistic. Impractical. Escapist. Depressive.

The Houses. The twelve houses represent areas of life experience. To stay with the example of the Moon, if it is placed in the part of the birth chart that represents home, the person feels most comfortable and secure in the familiarity and nurturance of family and the domestic environment. If the Moon is placed, instead, in the house of career and life direction, that person, seeks and finds an emotional connection to the public, in the outside world, and feels comfortable and secure in *that* environment.

· · ✦ THE HOUSES ✦ · ·

Number	Description	Negative Expression
1	Personality. Identity. How you interact with the world and the people in it.	Lack of self-assurance and self-confidence. Pessimism. Inhibition.
2	Values and priorities. Self-esteem. Security needs. Money and other material resources.	Materialism. Irresponsible use of resources. Self-limiting concerns about security. Low self-esteem.
3	Intellect. Communication. Early school experience. Siblings. Short-distance trips. The local environment or neighborhood.	Verbosity. Scattered attention. False intellectualism. Talking and not listening.
4	Early childhood experience. The domestic environment you create as an adult. Mom (i.e. the nurturing parent.) Roots. Your home.	Isolation. Insecurity. Not feeling grounded. A difficult relationship with the nurturing parent.
5	Creative self-expression. Your own children. Love affairs (that first great "three months" part). Recreation and pleasure. Risk-taking.	Unhealthy relationships. Creative blockage. Issues with your children. Recklessness.
6	Work (the day-to-day of it and how you do it.) Service. Duties. Health. Habits and routines. Pets.	Drudgery. Workaholism. Health challenges. Irresponsibility.

· · ✦ THE HOUSES ✦ · ·

Number	Description	Negative Expression
7	Partnership: personal, professional, and any other kind you can think of.	Fear of intimacy. Unequal relationships. Inability to form a stable bond.
8	Transformation. Empowerment. Deep, bonding sexuality. Resources held jointly with others. Issues of trust. The occult.	Blocked or excessive sexuality. Betrayal. Inordinate fear of death. Denial of world beyond that which can be seen. Irresponsible use of joint resources.
9	Higher education. The quest for meaning. Philosophy. Law. Ethics. Organized religion. Long-distance travel.	Rigidity of thought and beliefs. Unprincipled behavior. Wanderlust.
10	Your mission: what you are here to give to the world. Career and profession. Ambition. Interaction with the public. Dad (i.e. the authoritarian parent).	Lack of goals. Obsession with power and status. Sacrifice of personal life for career. Difficult relationships with authority figures.
11	Your hopes, dreams and wishes. The future. Groups. Friends and allies. Social consciousness. Harvest.	Vagueness of purpose. Problems with friendships. Not fitting in.
12	Spirituality. Mysticism. The unconscious and what is hidden there. Unrecognized strengths. Dreams. Seclusion.	Confusion. Escapism. Addiction. Drifting. Procrastination. Unrealized potential. The inner saboteur.

Putting it all together: Constructing the birth chart. Understanding how the birth chart is created can give insight into how the astrological symbols interact to form a picture of an individual's energetic make-up. However, this information, which is quite technical, is not at all necessary in order to get the most out of *Your Astrological Compass*.

Step One: Set up the houses and signs. Imagine two perfect 360° circles. One is drawn on white cardboard and divided into twelve numbered, pie-shaped segments of not necessarily equal size. A horizontal line crosses dead center from left to right. Segments numbered 1-6, in order, are arrayed in the lower half, starting at the left. Segments numbered 7-12, in order, are in the upper half, going from right to left. This is the birth chart, the 360° bowl of the sky, divided into the twelve houses that represent the areas of life's activities and experiences.

The second circle is constructed of clear plastic and also consists of 12 pie-shaped segments, but this time each piece is of equal size, taking up 30° of the 360° circle. Each segment is a different transparent color. These are the twelve signs.

Now, place the color-segmented transparent circle over the white cardboard one and secure them together with a paper clasp in dead center. Roughly speaking, that clasp is you, smack dab in the middle of your own birth chart and energy field. The white circle of houses is always in the same position for everyone, with the First House at the left, starting at the horizon line. The colored wheel can spin – one "spin" per lifetime – creating a pattern of signs that literally colors the activities and experiences associated with each of the houses. A house can actually have up to three signs "coloring" its landscape, but two is what's typical. The resulting imprint of sign on house is permanent and lasts for an entire lifetime.

The qualities of the sign overlaying each house in the birth chart influence the nature of the experiences represented by that house. Let's say that one of the segments in the color wheel is red, and let's say that red represents the sign of Aries. To keep our example simple, we're going to stipulate that the colored filter is completely covering the Sixth House, which represents, among other things, health. Aries is an energetic, enthusiastic fiery sign, full of physical vitality, and with those qualities filtering the nature of one's health, we can expect that the person will have a strong constitution, lots of energy and stamina, and will have a need to always be doing lots of physical activity to release that energy. It wouldn't be surprising to find a good number of Aries-in-the-Sixth-House people on the starting line for the New York Marathon or the *Tour de France*.

Let's change to another filter. Imagine blue this time, and associate that color with the sign of Pisces, a very different kind of energy. Pisces is a sensitive, intuitive, flowing water sign. With languid Pisces filtering the house of health, physical energy can be muted and laid-back, so the person needs to get a lot of rest and eat right to develop and maintain their stamina, and may need to hire a personal trainer to get themselves on the move.

Step Two: Place the planets where they belong. This is simpler than you might think. The planets move in regular patterns in their orbits against the background of the celestial belt of the twelve signs, which is called the zodiac. Because the planets are totally reliable and predictable in their movement, their actual physical positions can be precisely established for any moment forward and backward in time. Astrologers use this astronomical data to establish the planetary positions in the birth chart.

For example, Saturn's position on January 1, 2000 was at approximately 10° of the sign of Taurus. Simply find where the tenth degree of the sign of Taurus is located in the birth chart and place Saturn right there. That's it. Since there are twelve houses and only ten planets, not every house will have a planetary occupant.

Not so long ago it used to take a huge amount of the astrologer's time to manually set up the chart and see how it was being affected by the ongoing movement of the planets. Now, of course, it's done with a point and a click, but the underlying calculations and data sources have never changed. Astrological technique is totally reliable, but the astrologer has to be careful in this high-tech world. I once inadvertently created a chart for someone born in 1059 instead of 1959. The computer had no problem at all setting it up.

The interrelationship between planets, signs and houses that creates the perfect mandala of the birth chart results in a virtual infinity of combinations, which is why it takes 25,000 (yes, that's 25 plus three zeroes) years for the birth chart to duplicate itself in every detail. Still, like so much of the true magic and mystery of the world, behind its evident complexity lies exquisite simplicity, dependability, and meaning.

GLOSSARY

Aspect(s). Angular connections between the planets that describe the qualities of the energies that flow between the planets involved in the relationship. Aspects are calculated based on the number of degrees of distance (out of the 360 degrees in a circle) between the planets (usually, but not always, two) making up the aspect.

- *Conjunction.* A close gathering of two or more planets that are positioned right next to or on top of each other. Together, they combine to create an intense power point of energy.

- *Opposition.* Created by planets positioned approximately 180 degrees apart from one another. The energies flowing between them are opposite in nature, and so are not very comfortable, but achieving balance among them can result in great strength and growth.

- *Sextile.* Created by planets positioned approximately 60 degrees apart from each other. The combination creates a smooth flow of energy between the planets, but it is the energy of opportunity. That is, it must be recognized and used in order to have an effect.

- *Square.* Created by planets positioned approximately 90 degrees apart from one another. The energy flowing between them is uncomfortable, characterized by friction and tension, but the square can provide energy for growth and change.

- *Trine.* Created by planets positioned approximately 120 degrees apart from each other. The combination creates a smooth, natural, harmonious, strongly, positive flow of energy between the planets.

Baby Boomers, Boomers. Generational group born between approximately 1945 and 1964. In numbers, it constitutes the largest generation in America's history, and makes up about one-quarter to one-third of its current population.

Birth Chart, Horoscope. A circular graphic representation, divided into twelve sections, that depicts where the planets are positioned at the exact time and place of your birth.

Conjunction. See *Aspects.*

Cycle, Planetary. The amount of time it takes for a planet to pass through all twelve signs of the zodiac, complete the circuit of the birth chart and return to its original natal position.

- *Jupiter Cycle.* The Jupiter Cycle takes approximately 12 years.

- *Neptune Cycle.* The Neptune Cycle takes approximately 164 years.

- *Saturn Cycle.* The Saturn Cycle takes approximately 29 years.

- *Uranus Cycle.* The Uranus Cycle takes approximately 84 years.

Cycle of Adulthood. The period between the approximate ages of 30-59 during which we assume adult responsibilities and enjoy its privileges.

Cycle of Individuation. The eighty-four-year-long period of the Uranus Cycle that provides the opportunity to recognize and develop one's own unique authenticity and individuality.

Cycle of the Meaningful Return to the Self. The period, from approximately age sixty forward, when we live the life that reflects our own unique authenticity and potential.

Cycle of Preparation. The period between birth and approximately age twenty-nine, during which we acquire (or don't) the skills, experiences, and information we need in order to assume the full responsibilities and privileges of adulthood.

Generational Transits. Planetary passages that occur for everyone at a certain age in life, thereby influencing everyone born within a certain time frame.

Glyph. Graphic astrological symbol representing a planet or sign.

Greater Benefic. Classic astrological name for Jupiter, the planet representing good fortune, expansiveness, optimism, and abundance.

Grand Sextile. Planetary passage, occurring between the ages of 60-62, when each planet has come to a position where its energy is flowing smoothly back to itself in its unchanging natal position in the birth chart. The Grand Sextile provides an important energy refueling for the entire chart.

Horoscope. See **Birth Chart.**

House(s). Twelve pie-shaped segments of the perfectly circular field of the birth chart. Each represents certain areas of life experience. Thumbnail descriptions of what each house represents are found in **More About the Birth Chart** in this **Appendix.**

Kairos. The Greek word for the eternal present, time that *cannot* be measured by the clock.

Kronos. The Greek word for time as measured by the clock; the classic name for the planet Saturn.

Law of Attraction. The principle that thoughts and expectations influence experience; that what you focus on and believe in is what you manifest, or attract, into your life.

Mandala. A symbolic pattern or design, usually circular in shape, that graphically represents a depiction of the Universe.

Midlife Transits. Planetary energy passages that move through the birth chart of everyone between the approximate ages of 40-44.

Opposition. See *Aspects.*

Planet(s). Celestial bodies representing certain types of energy found in everyone. Thumbnail descriptions of what each planet represents is found in the **Planets** chart in Chapter 1.

Progression. Astrological calculation method that results in the creation of a meaningful relationship between one day of a planet's actual movement in its orbit, and one year of calendar time. Progressions are used to measure the evolutionary growth associated with the fast-moving personal planets (Sun, Moon, Mercury, Venus and Mars.)

Progressed Lunar Cycle (See *Cycle, Planetary* above.) The Moon's progressed cycle takes approximately twenty-eight years.

Return. The occasion of a planet arriving at its unchanging natal position in the birth chart, after traveling completely through the twelve signs of the zodiac. At return times, one cycle ends and another begins for the planet having the return.

Saturn Return. See *"Return."*

- *Saturn at Birth.* See *Cycle of Preparation.*

- *First Saturn Return.* See *Cycle of Adulthood.*

- *Second Saturn Return.* See *Cycle of the Meaningful Return to the Self.*

Sextile. See *Aspects.*

Sign(s). The twelve astrological signs (Aries, Taurus, Gemini, etc.) are filters that are applied to the planets' basic energies, modifying and "coloring" their expression. Thumbnail descriptions of the qualities of each sign are found in **More About the Birth Chart** in this **Appendix**.

Square. See *Aspects.*

Synchronicity. The circumstance where logically unrelated situations or events occur without apparent cause-and-effect connection, but convey real meaning that can be recognized by the observer.

Transit(s). Angular relationships created when a planet that is moving in its orbit makes an energetic connection to a natal planet that is sitting in its unchanging position in the birth chart. Transits make the same angles as aspects (See *Aspects*).

Trine. See *Aspects*.

Zodiac. The oval-shaped band of the twelve astrological signs through which the planets move in their orbits around the Sun.

BIBLIOGRAPHY

Arroyo, Stephen. *Exploring Jupiter. The Astrological Key to Progress, Prosperity and Potential.* USA: CRCS Publications, 1996

Arroyo, Stephen. *Relationships and Life Cycles.* USA: CRCS Publications, 1979

Borysenko, Joan. *A Woman's Book of Life. The Biology, Psychology, and Spirituality of the Feminine Life Cycle.* New York: Riverhead Books, 1996

Borysendo, Joan and Dveirin, Gordon. *Your Soul's Compass. What is Spiritual Guidance?* Carlsbad, CA: Hay House, 2007

Brussat, Frederic and Mary Ann. *Spiritual Literacy. Reading the Sacred in Everyday Life.* New York: Scribner, 1996

Celestial Fortune Cookie (The). New York: Viking Studio. Putnam Inc., 2000

Cheney, Karen. "Gift of a Lifetime." Washington, DC: *AARP Magazine,* September & October 2004

Clark, Brian. "The Aging of the Pluto in Leo Generation." Cedar Ridge, CA: *The Mountain Astrologer,* August/September 2001

Cousineau, Phil. *Once and Future Myths. The Power of Ancient Stories in Modern Times.* Berkeley, CA: Conari Press, 2001

Cunningham, Donna. *Healing Pluto Problems.* York Beach, ME: Samuel Weiser, 1986

Firak-Mitz, Phyllis. "Saturn: Our Personal Trainer for Excellence." Cedar Ridge, CA: *The Mountain Astrologer,* December/January 1998-1999

Firak-Mitz, Phyllis. "Uranus. Use your Genius to be Part of, Not

Apart From, Humanity." Cedar Ridge, CA: *The Mountain Astrologer*, August/September 1999

Forrest, Jodie. "Living with Uranus Transits." Cedar Ridge, CA: *The Mountain Astrologer*, February/March 2004

Forrest, Jodie. "Neptune: Where More than Two Worlds Touch." Cedar Ridge, CA: *The Mountain Astrologer*, February/March 2005

Forrest, Steven. *The Book of Pluto.* San Diego, CA: ACS Publications, 1994.

Forrest, Steven. *The Changing Sky.* San Diego, CA: ACS Publications, 1989.

Fulghum, Robert. *From Beginning to End. The Rituals of our Lives.* New York: Villard Books (Random House), 1995

Gerhardt, Dana. "Jupiter and Saturn." Cedar Ridge, CA: *The Mountain Astrologer*, February/March 2007

Gerhardt, Dana. "Neptune." Cedar Ridge, CA: *The Mountain Astrologer*, June/July 2007

Grasse, Ray. "Simple Rituals for Major Transits." Cedar Ridge, CA: *The Mountain Astrologer*, August/September 2000

Greene, Liz. *Saturn. A New Look at an Old Devil.* York Beach, ME: Samuel Weiser, 1976

Hand, Robert. *Planets in Transit. Life Cycles for Living.* West Chester, PA: Whitford Press, 1976.

Howell, Alice. *Jungian Symbolism in Astrology.* Wheaton, Il.: The Theosophical Publishing House, 1987.

LeShan, Eda. *It's Better to be Over the Hill Than Under It. Thoughts on Life over Sixty.* New York: Newmarket Press, 1990

Mitchel, Claire. *The Third Third.* Silver Spring, MD: Bartleby Press, 1991

Moore, Thomas. *Care of the Soul. A Guide for Cultivating Depth and Sacredness in Everyday Life.* New York: Harper Collins Publishers Inc., 1992

Morimando, Patricia. *The Neptune Effect.* York Beach, ME: Samuel Weiser, Inc., 1979

Ram Dass. *Still here. Embracing Aging, Changing, and Dying.* New York: Riverhead Books, 2000

Rubin, Lillian B. *Sixty on Up. The Truth about Aging in America.* Boston, MA: Beacon Press, 2007

Russo, Richard. *Bridge of Sighs.* New York: Alfred A. Knopf, 2007

Sheehy, Gail. *New Passages. Mapping Your Life Across Time.* New York: Random House, 1995

Spring, Elizabeth. "Using Neptune Homeopathically." Cedar Ridge, CA: *The Mountain Astrologer,* June/July 2009

Sullivan, Erin. *The Astrology of Midlife and Aging.* New York: Jeremy P. Tarcher/Penguin, 2005

Sullivan, Erin. *Saturn in Transit: Boundaries of Mind, Body and Soul.* London, England: Arkana/Penguin, 1991

Valeria, Andrea. *The Celestial Fortune Cookie: An Astrological Book of Days with Quotations for Every Sign.* New York: Viking Studio/ Penguin Putnam, Inc. 2000

Virtue, Doreen. *The Crystal Children: A guide to the Newest Generation of Psychic And Sensitive Children.* Carlsbad, California: Hay House Inc. 2003

CHAPTER NOTES

All references are in the Bibliography unless noted.

INTRODUCTION

Quoted in *Spiritual Literacy. Reading the Sacred in Everyday Life,* p. 260

CHAPTER 1

Quoted in *The Celestial Fortune Cookie*, p. 258

Forrest, Steven. *The Changing Sky*, p. 25

CHAPTER 2

Cousineau, Phil. *Once and Future Myths*, p. 169

CHAPTER 3

Quoted in *Spiritual Literacy. Reading the Sacred in Everyday Life,* p. 272

2 Sheehy, Gail. *New Passages: Mapping your Life Across Time*, p. 4

CHAPTER 5

Russo, Richard. *Bridge of Sighs,* p. 508

Mitchel, Claire. *The Third Third*, p. xi

Sheehy, Gail. *New Passages: Mapping your Life Across Time*, p. 326.

Borysenko, Joan. *A Woman's Book of Life: The Biology, Psychology, and Spirituality of the Feminine Life Cycle*, p. 210

Borysenko, Joan. *A Woman's Book of Life: The Biology, Psychology, and Spirituality of the Feminine Life Cycle*, p. 218

Sheehy, Gail. *New Passages: Mapping your Life Across Time*, p. 326.

Ram Dass. *Still Here. Embracing Aging, Changing and Dying*, p. 156

Russo, Richard. *Bridge of Sighs*, p. 516

Gerhardt, Dana. *Jupiter and Saturn*. The Mountain Astrologer, p. 10

PLANETARY PLAYBOOK

Borysenko, Joan and Dveirin, Gordon. *Your Soul's Compass. What is Spiritual Guidance?*, p. 126

AUTHOR PROFILE

ALICE LOFFREDO

In 1993 ALICE LOFFREDO LEFT A SUCCESSFUL CAREER AS A SYSTEMS manager for a major insurance company to follow the calling of her own birth chart and start an astrological consulting practice. She has taught astrology and tarot both for private students and the local community college, and is a popular lecturer at workshops, special interest groups, charity events, and bookstores. Her first book, *Perfect Together: Astrology, Karma and You*, was published inin 2008. She lives in central New Jersey with her husband Don and Dolly, the best rescue-cat ever.

You can learn more about Alice and her work by visiting
www.AstrologyKarmaAndYou.com

CPSIA information can be obtained at www.ICGtesting.com
Printed in the USA
BVOW03s0122141013

333583BV00001B/1/P